THE
MICHELIN
GUIDE

D1605877

CHICAGO

MICHELIN

THE MICHELIN GUIDE'S COMMITMENTS

Whether they are in Japan, the USA, China or Europe, our inspectors apply the same criteria to judge the quality of each and every establishment that they visit. The MICHELIN guide commands a **worldwide reputation** thanks to the commitments we make to our readers—and we reiterate these below:

Our inspectors make **anonymous visits** to restaurants to gauge the quality of cuisine offered to the everyday customer. They pay their own bill and make no indication of their presence. These visits are supplemented by comprehensive monitoring of information—our readers' comments are one valuable source, and are always taken into consideration.

Our choice of establishments is a completely **independent** one, made for the benefit of our readers alone. Decisions are discussed by the inspectors and editor, with the most important considered at the global level. Inclusion in the Guide is always free of charge.

The Guide offers a **selection** of the best restaurants in each category of comfort and price. A recommendation in the Guide is an honor in itself, and defines the establishment among the "best of the best."

All practical information, the classifications, and awards are revised and updated every year to ensure the most **reliable information** possible.

The standards and criteria for the classifications are the same in all countries covered by the MICHELIN guides. Our system is used worldwide and easy to apply when selecting a restaurant.

As part of Michelin's ongoing commitment to improving **travel and mobility**, we do everything possible to make vacations and eating out a pleasure.

THE MICHELIN GUIDE'S SYMBOLS

Michelin inspectors are experts at finding the best restaurants and invite you to explore the diversity of the gastronomic universe. As well as evaluating a restaurant's cooking, we also consider its décor, the service and the ambience – in other words, the all-round culinary experience.

Two keywords help you make your choice more quickly: red for the type of cuisine, gold for the atmosphere.

Italian • Elegant

FACILITIES & SERVICES

🍇	Notable wine list
🍹	Notable cocktail list
🍺	Notable beer list
🍶	Notable sake list
BYO	Bring your own
♿	Wheelchair accessible
⛱	Outdoor dining
⟨⟩	Private dining room
☕	Breakfast
🥐	Brunch
🥢	Dim sum
🚗	Valet parking
💵	Cash only

AVERAGE PRICES

$	Under $25
$$	$25 to $50
$$$	$50 to $75
$$$$	Over $75

STARS

Our famous one ✿, two ✿✿ and three ✿✿✿ stars
identify establishments serving the highest quality
cuisine – taking into account the quality of ingredients,
the mastery of techniques and flavors, the levels of
creativity and, of course, consistency.

✿✿✿ Exceptional cuisine, worth a special journey
✿✿   Excellent cuisine, worth a detour
✿   High quality cooking, worth a stop

BIB GOURMAND

Good quality at a good value.

MICHELIN PLATE

Good cooking.
Fresh ingredients, capably
prepared: simply a good meal.

DEAR READER,

It is with great pleasure that we present the 2020 edition of the MICHELIN guide to Chicago. Over the past year, our inspectors have extended their reach to include a variety of establishments and multiplied their anonymous visits in order to accurately reflect the rich culinary diversity this great city has to offer.

Chicago has a wealth of dining choices at every turn. The city's history and culture have contributed to an intriguing and diverse selection—ranging from all-day breakfast cafés, iconic deep-dish pizza destinations, burly steakhouses and cutting-edge dining rooms. Every establishment has been chosen first and foremost for the quality of its cooking.

As part of the Guide's highly confidential and meticulous evaluation process, our inspectors who are expertly trained professionals in the food industry dine and drink as "everyday" customers. Therefore, they are able to experience and evaluate the same level of cuisine and service as any other guest.

Our company's founders, Édouard and André Michelin, published the first MICHELIN guide in 1900, to provide motorists with useful information about where they could service and repair their cars as well as find a good quality meal. In 1926, the star-rating system was introduced, whereby outstanding establishments are awarded for excellence in cuisine.

We take consumer feedback seriously. You may contact us at: michelin.guides@michelin.com and follow our Inspectors on Twitter (@MichelinGuideCH) as well as Instagram (@michelininspectors). We thank you for your patronage and hope that the MICHELIN guide will remain your preferred reference to Chicago's restaurants.

CONTENTS

CHICAGO

Mlenny/iStock

EATING IN...
ANDERSONVILLE, EDGEWATER & UPTOWN

Chicago's North side is rich with culinary traditions from centuries of immigrant settlers. A water tower emblazoned with the blue-and-yellow Swedish flag rises above Clark Street, proudly representing Andersonville's Nordic roots. Early birds line up for coffee and breakfast (sassy eggs, anyone?) at **Over Easy Café**, while heartier appetites won't be able to resist the Viking breakfast at **Svea Restaurant**, featuring Swedish-style pancakes, sausages, and toasted limpa bread. Later, visit the Swedish-American Museum for a history lesson. This area also brings the world to its doorstep thanks to those stocked shelves at **Middle East Bakery & Grocery**. However, if your tastes run south (of the border), then **Isabella Bakery** is a gem for all things Guatemalan. Across town, the pagoda-style roof of the Argyle El stop on the Red Line serves as another visual clue to the plethora of eats—an East Asian lineup of Chinese, Thai, and Vietnamese restaurants, noodle shops, and more. Lacquered, bronzed duck and pork make **Sun Wah BBQ** a popular spot for Cantonese cuisine, while **dak** is beloved for spicy chicken wings and rice bowls. **BopNgrill** specializes in Asian fusion food like loco moco and a kimchi burger.

German immigrants helped develop Lincoln Square and their appreciation for fine meats still resonates here. Old-time butchers ply their trade, stuffing wursts and offering specialty meats at **Gene's Sausage Shop**. For a more refined selection, head to **Lincoln Quality Meat Market**. Speaking of meat treats, **Wolfy's** serves one of the best red-hots. There is a

farmer's market to be found in the area most days of the week, but the Wednesday **Andersonville Farmer's Market** is beloved for its bakeries and array of Asian fruit. **Lincoln Square Farmer's Market** throws its doors open on Tuesdays, while **HarvesTime Foods** is a culinary bazaar focused on sustainability.

Edgewater's Sauce and Bread Kitchen, a collaboration between beloved artisans Co-op Sauce and Crumb Chicago, brings two favorite local products together. Critically acclaimed as one of the country's best boutique coffee shops, **The Coffee Studio** pours a mean cup of joe, bested with their "glazed & infused" doughnuts. Creative types convene at **The Metropolis Café**, an offshoot of Chicago's own **Metropolis Coffee Company**; but if craving something stronger than caffeine, **Independent Spirits Inc.** is a wine and liquor shop replete with global selections from family-owned and small-batch producers.

ANDERSONVILLE, & UPTOWN

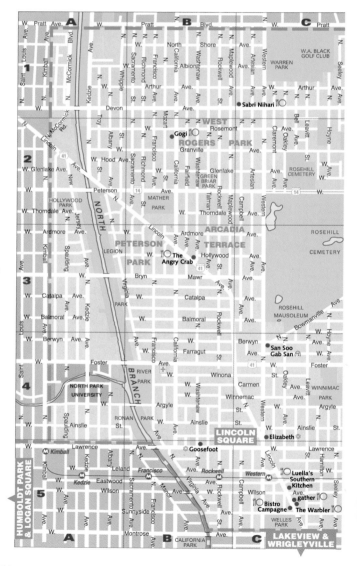

EDGEWATER

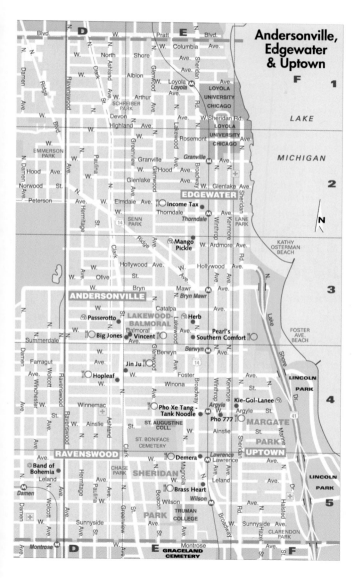

Andersonville,
Edgewater
& Uptown

LAKE
MICHIGAN

EDGEWATER

ANDERSONVILLE

LAKEWOOD
BALMORAL

RAVENSWOOD

SHERIDAN

UPTOWN

MARGATE
PARK

LINCOLN
PARK

FOSTER
AVE.
BEACH

KATHY
OSTERMAN
BEACH

CLARENDON
PARK

TRUMAN
COLLEGE

PARK
COLLEGE

GRACELAND
CEMETERY

ST. BONIFACE
CEMETERY

ST. AUGUSTINE
COLL.

LOYOLA
UNIVERSITY
CHICAGO

LOYOLA
UNIVERSITY
CHICAGO

SCHREIBER
PARK

SENN
PARK

CHASE
PARK

EMMERSON
PARK

LANE
PARK

Income Tax
Mango
Pickle
Herb
Pearl's
Southern Comfort
Passerotto
Big Jones
Vincent
Jin Ju
Hopleaf
Pho Xe Tang -
Tank Noodle
Pho 777
Kie-Gol-Lanee
Demera
Band of
Bohemia
Brass Heart

THE ANGRY CRAB ⅃○

Seafood • Simple

♿ **BYO**

MAP: B3

If there were ever a restaurant that demands bringing at least one friend along, it's this one. Lines form nightly for the chance to fill up on a Cajun-style spread, and guests are required to order at least one total pound of seafood that includes the likes of crawfish, whole head-on shrimp, and snow crab legs.

Pick from a choice of lemon, garlic, or spicy sauces; stake your claim on a roll of paper towels; and feast upon your selection, which arrives hot in plastic bags. One look around the room and you'll see that silverware is a second-thought, as most are digging in with their sleeves rolled up and their hands at the ready. Still hungry? Make it a true crab boil and add sausage, corn on the cob, as well as red bliss potatoes to round out the feast.

■ 5665 N. Lincoln Ave. (bet. Fairfield & Washtenaw Aves.)
☏ (773) 784-6848 — **WEB:** www.theangrycrabchicago.com
■ Closed Monday - Friday lunch   **PRICE:** $$

BIG JONES ⅃○

Southern • Bistro

MAP: E3

Boasting a refreshed interior and an open kitchen equipped with extra gadgets, this big kid on the block greets guests with barrel-aged punch selections, as well as an impressive list of Bourbon and whiskey. From its cookbook collection to brocade walls lined with portraits of life in the South, the place oozes warmth and is a guaranteed good time. Yes, it's no front porch in Louisiana, but it's certainly close.

The menu too is rooted in the South, but as often as the chef trots out his grandmother's heirloom recipes, he dishes out creative tweaks, many with Mexican influences. Cheddar-corn fritters with a chili pepper-vinegar dip and bread pudding are staples, while the hen and hominy presents a south-of-the-border slant on chicken and dumplings.

■ 5347 N. Clark St. (bet. Balmoral & Summerdale Aves.)
▤ Berwyn
☏ (773) 275-5725 — **WEB:** www.bigjoneschicago.com
■ Open lunch & dinner daily   **PRICE:** $$

BAND OF BOHEMIA ✿

Gastropub • Rustic

So much more than a working brewery with a talented kitchen, Band of Bohemia is in fact a truly inspired gastropub that produces its own utterly unique creations both in the glass and on the plate.

Located in a repurposed brick building across from the Metra tracks, the look is unapologetically industrial with an expansive layout that unwinds into a series of seating options, inviting bar, and an open kitchen with another small bar set against pretty blue tiles. Curved, high-backed booths lend intimacy to counter the room's sheer size. Stainless steel tanks displayed in the back hold the culinary-minded handiwork of their head brewer. On tap, expect a handful of rotating beers.

The kitchen's boundless small and large plates defy expectations with delicious success. Scallop ceviche straddles the line between sweet and sour courtesy of chartreuse, candied ginger, and roast shishito peppers. Who knew a single carrot could have such power? Salt-cured, roasted, and glazed in miso caramel, then set upon beluga lentils and creamy coconut milk—it's a revelation. The creativity continues through dessert, with unconventional pairings like the tangy and sweet dill crème fraîche ice cream.

■ 4710 N. Ravenswood Ave. (bet. Lawrence & Leland Aves.)

🚇 Damen (Brown)

☎ (773) 271-4710 — **WEB:** www.bandofbohemia.com

■ Closed Monday, Tuesday - Friday lunch   **PRICE: $$$**

ANDERSONVILLE, EDGEWATER & UPTOWN

BISTRO CAMPAGNE
French • Bistro

MAP: C5

The romantic ideal of a French bistro is alive and well at quaint Bistro Campagne, where a tiny bar by the entrance is ready with your aperitif. Light slants through wooden Venetian blinds, bouncing off cream-and-brick walls in the welcoming dining room. Choose a white cloth-covered table inside or dine outside under the garden's twinkling lights and green tree branches.

Inspired accompaniments make for memorable versions of rustic French standards. Start with a large, savory bowl of soupe à l'oignon gratinée capped with a thick layer of melting Gruyère. Then, discover their pitch-perfect duck pithiviers, wild mushroom duxelles and hazelnuts in puff pastry with a Madeira reduction. Brown butter pain perdu tucked with black figs is moist and delicious.

- 4518 N. Lincoln Ave. (bet. Sunnyside & Wilson Aves.)
- Western (Brown)
- (773) 271-6100 — **WEB:** www.bistrocampagne.com
- Closed Monday - Saturday lunch   **PRICE: $$**

BRASS HEART
Contemporary • Elegant

MAP: E5

With only 20 seats, this tasting-menu retreat is serious yet intimate, boasting marble-topped tables, plush seating, and glamorous gold accents. But it has a playful spirit as well, as seen in the black-and-white portraits of Lollapalooza alumni that line the walls. Across both omnivorous and vegan prix-fixe menus, Chef/partner Matt Kerney displays a tongue-in-cheek wit to his creations. Find evidence of this in his potato-chip ice cream, which mysteriously evokes a classic bag of Lay's with added zing from bursts of Osetra caviar. Pristine spring pea soup gets extra flavor from a sausage-stuffed rabbit loin and coins of pickled carrots.

Finally, a dash of yuzu brightens luscious scallops in beurre blanc. It's a cool, clever twist on contemporary fare.

- 4662 N. Broadway (at Clifton Ave.)
- Lawrence
- (773) 564-9680 — **WEB:** brassheartrestaurant.com
- Closed Sunday - Monday, Tuesday - Saturday lunch
          PRICE: $$$$

18

DEMERA 🍴

Ethiopian • Simple

 ♿

MAP: E5

Demera's well-lit corner location welcomes hungry Uptown residents looking to immerse themselves in Ethiopian cuisine. Colorful wicker seating at the dining room's communal table gives groups an authentic experience, while picture windows offer plenty of people-watching for everyone.

Vegetarian and omnivorous offerings abound on the menu, which also features a small glossary of terms to help newcomers. Pleasantly spicy yesiga wot combines tender chunks of beef with onions and ginger in a rich berbere sauce. Served with turmeric-infused split peas and spicy jalapeño-laced collard greens, this stew is a hearty pleasure. Sop up the extra sauce with piles of tangy and soft injera, presented in the traditional manner in lieu of silverware.

▪ 4801 N. Broadway (at Lawrence Ave.)

🚇 Lawrence

☎ (773) 334-8787 — **WEB:** www.demeraethiopian.com

▪ Open lunch & dinner daily

PRICE: $$

GATHER 🍴

American • Neighborhood

 ♿   🪑   🍽   📖

MAP: C5

A chic, cozy space lets guests get up close and personal at gather. Diners seeking dinner and a show take front row seats at barstools lining the open kitchen's polished granite counter, while tall communal tables fill with patrons enjoying bites from the menu's "gather and share" section. A rear dining room offers more solitude and romance.

Family-style Sunday dinners are a local draw, but the à la carte menu showcases flavorful options nightly. Slice into a single large uovo raviolo to mingle poached egg and ricotta with white truffle butter, jalapeño slivers and chopped chives, or share a crock of Pernod-splashed mussels. Fragrant and garlicky, they're served with sourdough toast points for soaking up every last drop of the white wine-cream sauce.

▪ 4539 N. Lincoln Ave. (bet. Sunnyside & Wilson Aves.)

🚇 Western (Brown)

☎ (773) 506-9300 — **WEB:** www.gatherchicago.com

▪ Closed Monday - Friday lunch

PRICE: $$

ELIZABETH ✿
Contemporary • Cozy

MAP: C4

Chef Iliana Regan's unique approach to cooking at her popular Elizabeth is self-described as "New Gatherer" cuisine. Hunting and foraging are star features of this local, seasonal menu, and though her multi-course menu changes nightly (sometimes leading to subtle variations in quality) she consistently utilizes ingredients in ways that push the envelope. As proof of her talent, her popular cooking classes regularly sell out, even at $1,000 a pop.

Tucked into a bright interior, festooned with dried branches, river rocks, antlers and pottery, the décor alters with the menu. But the highlight of the space remains its fully open kitchen. Likewise, service is cheerful, warm and attentive, if a touch casual at times.

Dinner is likely to be an earthy ten—albeit manageable—course affair, and might begin with a creamy scoop of wildly fresh cheese set over sorel mushroom purée and topped with a cloud of elderflower foam, spruce shoots and foraged plant bulbs. Later, a bread service featuring soft goat butter, crisp pork cracklings and luscious whipped lardo is memorable to say the least. At the end, a knob of turbot reaches striking new heights dressed with beurre monté and crunchy white asparagus.

■ 4835 N. Western, Unit D (bet. Ainslie St. & Lawrence Ave.)
▣ Western (Brown)
☎ (773) 681-0651 — **WEB:** www.elizabeth-restaurant.com
■ Closed Sunday - Monday, Tuesday - Saturday lunch

PRICE: $$$$

GOGI ⅋⚬

Korean • Neighborhood

MAP: B2

The surging popularity of Korean food continues to flourish along these shores of Lake Michigan. And as foodies would have you know, Gogi is one of the best places in the city to experience it. With its hip, industrial décor, imposing exhaust fans over each table (a clear sign that there's a ton of grilling going on) and lively blend of sweet, spicy and sour flavors, dinner here promises to be a sensory explosion like no other.

One could feast on the abundant pre-meal banchan alone—a stunning selection of kimchi, mirin-soaked fish cakes, sake-steamed black beans and more. But, that would mean missing out on delicate slices of sirloin bulgogi smothered in a sweet, gingery marinade; or restorative and spicy sundubu jjigae bubbling away in an iron pot.

■ 6240 N. California Ave. (bet. Granville & Rosemont Aves.)
℗ (773) 274-6669 — **WEB:** www.gogichicago.com
■ Closed lunch daily

PRICE: $$

HERB 😊

Thai • Contemporary Décor

BYO

MAP: E3

In the sea of Thai restaurants that flank this area, elegant Herb stands out for its lovely wood and stone décor and service staff friendly enough to use your name. This is killer food, elevated and prepared with care.

The kitchen turns out both a three- and five-course prix-fixe dinner at tremendous value, but Chef/owner Patty Neumson's cooking is light (and delicious) enough to go the distance. A sample menu might begin with a cool pile of crunchy green papaya, carrot and cucumber, laced in a beautifully balanced lime dressing with vermicelli noodles and peanuts. Then move on to tofu and kabocha in a deliciously complex coconut curry full of wilted basil and heat. Soft glass noodles find their match in sautéed onions, fresh crab and crunchy shrimp.

■ 5424 N. Broadway (bet. Balmoral & Catalpa Aves.)
🚇 Bryn Mawr
℗ (773) 944-9050 — **WEB:** www.herbrestaurant.com
■ Closed Monday - Wednesday, Thursday - Sunday lunch

PRICE: $$

GOOSEFOOT ✿

Contemporary • Chic

 &♿ BYO

MAP: B5

This understated plate-glass façade may seem lost in a sea of mediocrity, but the restaurant it houses is truly distinct. The soothing décor appears minimal, with splashes of orange from the seating, bare tables, and Rodin replicas for an instantly likeable space. A small painting purchased by the chef and his wife on their honeymoon in Italy graces one corner of the room. Dishes are intricate and take time to be described, which may explain the relatively slow pace of dining here.

The menu showcases classical edge and contemporary artistry. Begin with a bowl of creamy pumpkin soup, where fresh bits of crab and pheasant sausage add a gumbo-like quality and smoked paprika kicks it up. Keep the comfort food mood going with a bowl of tortellini served in a brodo of parmesan, pecorino, and Burgundy truffles. Finally, a single diver scallop proves that one is not the loneliest number with its delicate hint of sweetness courtesy of the lobster, coconut and lemongrass-scented sauce.

Just when you think it couldn't possibly get any sweeter, the Goosefoot experience ends with handcrafted chocolates, a packet of seeds for your garden and a warm send-off from Chef Chris Nugent and his wife, Nina.

■ 2656 W. Lawrence Ave. (bet. Talman & Washtenaw Aves.)

🚇 Rockwell

📞 (773) 942-7547 — **WEB:** www.goosefoot.net

■ Closed Sunday - Tuesday, Wednesday - Saturday lunch

PRICE: $$$$

HOPLEAF 🍴

Gastropub • Tavern

MAP: D4

For over 25 years, Hopleaf has embodied that true Chicago tavern spirit, thanks to its refreshing lack of attitude, warm hospitality, and approachable cooking. A traditional bar graces the front, but the glassed-in kitchen is where the magic happens. Named after a pale ale brewed in Malta, this watering hole fittingly flaunts a beer list so long that it's been called "a novel."

Mussels are available night and day and arrive in your choice of an herbed white wine broth or a Belgian-style beer broth. Both preparations include a cone of crisp, house-made French fries. The duck breast Rueben is another solid choice, though you should save room for the lemon thyme pound cake, embellished with brown sugar-whipped mascarpone and a blueberry-tarragon compote.

◼ 5148 N. Clark St. (bet. Foster Ave. & Winona St.)
🚉 Berwyn
☎ (773) 334-9851 — **WEB:** www.hopleaf.com
◼ Open lunch & dinner daily

PRICE: $$

INCOME TAX 🍴

Contemporary • Elegant

MAP: E2

This versatile neighborhood haunt is cherished by couples on date night as well as happy hour types hanging out at the long bar for cocktails and bites. Decorated with handsome wood floors, globe lights, and windows letting in a flood of sunlight, the vibe inside is welcoming and manages to ease all moods.

Over in the kitchen, seasonal ingredients star in elegant bistro staples. Imagine the likes of citrus-cured sea trout or roasted cabbage presented with the leaves fanned out, each one garnished with toasty breadcrumbs and a delicious blend of garlic, fish sauce, and Calabrian chili oil. Close out with tender and juicy pork coppa laid atop a bed of fava beans and charred scallions—all tossed in spicy salsa verde. Sounds too delicious to pass up? It is.

◼ 5959 N. Broadway (bet. Elmdale & Thorndale Aves.)
🚉 Thorndale
☎ (773) 897-9165 — **WEB:** www.incometaxbar.com
◼ Closed Sunday - Monday, Tuesday - Saturday lunch

PRICE: $$$

23

JIN JU
Korean • Simple

MAP: E4

A sexy spot on a bustling stretch of North Clark, Jin Ju spins out luscious Korean classics with aplomb. Inside, dim lighting, dark wood furnishings and luxuriant fuchsia walls create a sophisticated coziness, while servers are gracious and attentive.

A simply named house salad showcases the restaurant's modern, accessible ethos, combining meaty pan-seared portobello strips atop delicately bitter green leaf lettuce, torn sesame leaves, cucumbers and scallions in a funky garlic-soy sauce. Without tableside barbecue grills, fatty pork slabs are sautéed in the kitchen for sweetly caramelized samgyupsal. Wrapped in sesame leaves with Brussels sprouts, beets, crispy leeks and a smear of kicky miso paste, the package provides instant gratification.

- 5203 N. Clark St. (at Foster Ave.)
- Berwyn
- (773) 334-6377 — **WEB:** www.jinjurestaurant.com
- Closed Monday, Tuesday - Sunday lunch

PRICE: $$

KIE-GOL-LANEE
Mexican • Simple

MAP: F4

If you think you know what to order from this kitchen because you've been to Oaxaca, just wait a minute and listen to your fellow diners. They too have made the journey and their knowledge could probably draw a map of the city. Located in the heart of Little Saigon, this quiet restaurant has been thriving thanks to a clientele who knows quality when they taste it.

The likes of soft, just-steamed pork tamales with a delicately spiced green mole; or wide, crackly tlayudas piled high with chorizo are presented to your table with the utmost care. The focused menu may have a number of highlights but one favorite is the Cornish hen roasted until its skin is crisp as a chip and then smothered with a dark, faintly sweet mole made from a riot of layered spices.

- 5004 N. Sheridan Rd. (at Argyle St.)
- Argyle
- (872) 241-9088 — **WEB:** kiegol.com
- Closed Monday - Friday lunch

PRICE: $$

LUELLA'S SOUTHERN KITCHEN 🍴

Southern • Family

♿ 🍷 BYO

MAP: C5

Don't be fooled by the no-frills interior of this homey little soul food spot. Yes, you order at the counter; and yes, you'll be helping yourself to utensils, napkins and ice water. However, Luella's is cooking up anything but fast food. This earnest kitchen makes your order from scratch, and it's more than worth the wait. The surrounding artwork is half the fun anyway: you might even recognize prints like "Sugar Shack" by artist Ernie Barnes from the 1970's sitcom, "Good Times. "

The tender buttermilk-fried chicken is a thing of beauty, served with warm collards braised with ham hock. Then pillowy biscuits, cooked to order and served with apricot jam, are pure bliss; as are Mississippi hot tamales stuffed with Slagel Farms beef and melted cheddar cheese.

- 4609 N. Lincoln Ave. (bet. Eastwood & Wilson Aves.)
- Western (Brown)
- (773) 961-8196 — **WEB:** www.luellassouthernkitchen.com
- Closed Monday - Friday lunch

PRICE: $$

MANGO PICKLE 😊

Indian • Colorful

MAP: E3

After traveling across India, Chef Marisa Paolillo was sufficiently inspired to return stateside and open a restaurant that celebrates its culinary diversity. Named for the country's most popular condiment, everything here—from the colorful artwork to the rich curries—shows a deep appreciation for the sub-continent.

The well-priced tasting offers an array of specialties. There is also a spring à la carte as well as a seven-course prix-fixe. Regardless of your pick, expect flavorful dishes that are a riff on the classics. Think of the onion-tomato sauce of butter chicken, ramped up with mushrooms and sundried tomatoes for a Mediterranean twist. Chana masala is spiked with ginger and garlic, while beef nihari spotlights a succulent black cardamom sauce.

- 5842 N. Broadway (bet. Rosedale Ave. & Victoria St.)
- Thorndale
- (773) 944-5555 — **WEB:** www.mangopicklechicago.com
- Closed Monday - Tuesday, Wednesday - Sunday lunch

PRICE: $$

PASSEROTTO ☺

Korean • Contemporary Décor

  ♿   **MAP:** D3

Cavatelli, cantuccini and crudos line the menu, but wait, isn't this a Korean restaurant? Indeed, the window advertises "fun Korean fare." However, Chef/owner Jennifer Kim honed her skills in Italian kitchens, so expect a cultural collision. It's a delightful surprise, one that welcomes a steady stream of area dwellers who arrive hungry for bright, bold and creative flavors—as seen in the Cacciucco-inspired tofu stew. Bay scallop crudo with a house-made XO sauce is another prime example of this Italian-Korean mashup. Then, pan-fried rice cakes with a lamb ragù hint at gnocchi, while Pelicana chicken is delicately fried and coated with a sweet and sticky red pepper glaze.

Despite Kim's sky-high creativity, the prices remain pleasantly down-to-earth.

◾ 5420 N. Clark St. (bet. Balmoral & Catalpa Aves.)

🚇 Bryn Mawr

📞 (708) 607-2102 — **WEB:** www.passerottochicago.com

◾ Closed Sunday - Monday, Tuesday - Saturday lunch   **PRICE:** $$

PEARL'S SOUTHERN COMFORT 🍴

Southern • Tavern

  ▢ ♿ 🌳 🛋   **MAP:** E3

Chicago's been on a Southern food kick of late, and this sparkling Andersonville charmer is a straight up hepcat. Its enormous arched windows open up to a completely revamped 100-year-old room, featuring long exposed ceiling beams, whitewashed brick, dark slate walls and soft leather chairs.

But even with all that design swag, the main draw at Pearl's Southern Comfort is still the food. For starters, there's the ace barbecue, but guests should hardly stop there. Try the enormous double cut pork chop, grilled to supple perfection and paired with "dirty" farro salad, Cajun slaw and pork jus. Another staple, the Louisiana jambalaya, is served decadently dark and spicy, brimming with tender chicken, Andouille sausage and Crystal hot sauce.

◾ 5352 N. Broadway (bet. Balmoral & Berwyn Aves.)

🚇 Berwyn

📞 (773) 754-7419 — **WEB:** www.pearlschicago.com

◾ Closed Monday - Friday lunch   **PRICE:** $$

PHO 777 🍴

Vietnamese • Simple

MAP: E4

A market's worth of fresh ingredients allows Pho 777 to stand out in a neighborhood where Vietnamese restaurants—and their signature soup—seem to populate every storefront. Bottles of hot sauce, jars of fiery condiments and canisters of spoons and chopsticks clustered on each table make it easy for regulars to sit down and start slurping.

Add choices like meatballs, tendon, flank steak and tofu to the cardamom- ginger- and clove-spiced beef broth, which fills a vat large enough to sate a lumberjack-sized appetite. Then throw in jalapeños, Thai basil and mint to your liking. If you're not feeling like pho this time around, snack on spring rolls with house-made roasted peanut sauce; or a stack of lacy bánh xèo stuffed with pork, chili sauce and sprouts.

■ 1063-65 W. Argyle St. (bet. Kenmore & Winthrop Aves.)
🚇 Argyle
℘ (773) 561-9909
■ Closed Monday

PRICE: $

PHO XE TANG - TANK NOODLE 🍴

Vietnamese • Simple

♿ BYO

MAP: E4

A stone's throw from the Little Saigon EL, this simple corner spot keeps pho enthusiasts coming back for more. Communal cafeteria-style tables, crowded during prime meal times, are stocked with all the necessary funky and spicy condiments. Efficient service keeps the joint humming and lets the patrons focus on slurping.

Pho is the definitive draw here, and this fragrant, five-spiced, rice noodle- and beef-filled broth is accompanied by sprouts, lime wedges and plenty of basil. Other delights on the massive menu include shrimp- and pork-stuffed rice flour rolls with spicy and sour nuoc cham. Follow that with a fiery catfish soup simmered with an intriguing combination of okra, pineapple and crunchy bamboo shoots drizzled with garlic oil.

■ 4953-55 N. Broadway (at Argyle St.)
🚇 Argyle
℘ (773) 878-2253 — **WEB:** www.tank-noodle.com
■ Closed Wednesday

PRICE: $

SABRI NIHARI 🍴

Indian • Family

 ♿

Outshining its competition on this stretch of West Devon Avenue, make your way inside this vast and massively posh South Asian hot spot, where crystal chandeliers make tangerine-hued walls gleam with glory. Unsurprisingly, vegetarian and deep-fried dishes abound, but that's only the beginning of the diverse, group-friendly menu. Nibble on crispy vegetable pakoras before moving on to the frontier chicken coupled with a buttery, baby blanket-sized naan. While most items skew Indian, it would be remiss to skip the namesake Pakistani signature—sabri nihari—starring slow-cooked and spicy stewed beef. Creamy lassi with homemade yogurt helps balance out the spice-fest.

No alcohol is served in deference to many of the abstaining clientele, but you won't miss it.

◼ 2500-2502 W. Devon Ave. (at Campbell Ave.)

☎ (773) 465-3272 — **WEB:** www.sabrinihari.com

◼ Open lunch & dinner daily   PRICE: $

SAN SOO GAB SAN 😊

Korean • Family

Tucked into a tiny strip mall in the West Edgewater-Upper Andersonville area, San Soo Gab San has generated quite a buzz among serious Korean food fans. Inside, you'll find a warm, welcoming space with large tabletop grills to cook your own meats.

Most excitingly, the authentic, traditional dishes turned out of the kitchen don't bow or cater to Western sensibilities—to wit, an incredibly flavorful bowl of piping hot goat meat soup arrives with wild sesame leaves and a flutter of seeds. Among the many popular casseroles and stews, don't miss the beoseot doenjang jjigae, chockablock with tender tofu, savory mushrooms, beef and veggies. The delicious barbecue is perfect for a group feast or those looking to have some fun with their food.

◼ 5247 N. Western Ave. (at Berwyn Ave.)

🚇 Western (Brown)

☎ (773) 334-1589 — **WEB:** www.ssgsbbq.com

◼ Open lunch & dinner daily   PRICE: $$

VINCENT 🍴

Belgian • Bistro

MAP: E3

Go Dutch at Vincent, where innovative yet approachable cooking meets a tried-and-true European bistro menu, boasting enough cheese to satisfy even the pickiest turophile. Adding to the romance, high-top marble tables and brocade-papered walls make for a warm, intimate ambience that's accented by tall votive candles.

Got an appetite? An overflowing pot of P. E. I. mussels is a decadent meal on its own, brimming with bits of pork belly, chilies, scallions and cilantro, accompanied by a big bowl of traditional frites with mayonnaise. Basil and lemon balm perk up risotto with charred purple cauliflower and braised fennel. Also, you'll want to hold on to your fork for slices of lemon butter cake with Chantilly cream and blueberry compote.

◼ 1475 W. Balmoral Ave. (bet. Clark St. & Glenwood Ave.)
🚇 Berwyn
📞 (773) 334-7168 — **WEB:** www.vincentchicago.com
◼ Closed Monday, Tuesday - Saturday lunch

PRICE: $$

THE WARBLER 🍴

American • Chic

MAP: C5

All neighborhood restaurants should aspire to be more like The Warbler. This latest venture from the team behind gather is located just next door, and features a dining room that is far more sleek and contemporary than you might expect. Yet it remains as comfy as ever, helping it become an instant staple.

The playful cooking clearly shows effort as seen in their house-made pastas and artistic plating, but is always accessible and appealing. Chitarra twirled around blistered tomatoes in a buttery garlic sauce with shrimp are not only delicious but reasonably priced. The menu is also full of American classics like wings, nachos and flatbreads, but save room for desserts—like a carrot cake drenched in so much toffee sauce, it may as well be called a pudding.

◼ 4535 N. Lincoln Ave. (bet. Sunnyside & Wilson Aves.)
🚇 Western (Brown)
📞 (773) 681-0950 — **WEB:** www.thewarblerchicago.com
◼ Closed lunch daily

PRICE: $$

EATING IN...
BUCKTOWN
& WICKER PARK

Like many of the Windy City's neighborhoods, Bucktown and Wicker Park has seen their residents shift—from waves of Polish immigrants and wealthy families (who've erected stately mansions on Hoyne and Pierce avenues) to young folk introducing modern taquerias and craft breweries to these streets. Far from the globally known boutiques on Magnificent Mile, indie shops and artisan producers on Milwaukee and Damen avenues offer one-of-a-kind treasures for all five senses. Get a taste of Wicker Park's underground music scene at Reckless Records or music events, including the Wicker Park Fest, held each July.

It's a well-known saying that you don't want to know how the sausage is made, but the person who coined this phrase clearly never tasted the bounty from **Vienna Beef Factory**. Their popular workshop tour leaves visitors yearning for a 1/3-pound Mike Ditka Polish sausage at the café, or even a make-your-own-Chicago-dog kit from the gift shop. For more Eastern European fun, **Rich's Deli** is Ukrainian Village's go-to market for copious cuts of smoked pork, kabanosy, pasztet, Polish vodka, and Slavic mustard.

Hand-crafted goodies make this region a rewarding destination for sweets. Retro in vibe, the seasonal slices and small-town vibe of **Hoosier Mama Pie Company** brings old-time charm to this part of Chicago Avenue. From tiered wedding cakes to replicas of Wrigley Field, a tempting selection of desserts is displayed in the window at **Alliance Bakery**. But, if you're looking for something a little less traditional, unusual combos are the norm at **Black Dog Gelato**, where goat cheese, cashew,

and caramel come together for a great scoop. The craft beer movement has been brewing in Chicagoland for some time now, and, the noted beer school at Wicker Park's **Map Room** gives students a greater appreciation for the art—though a self-taught tour of the bar's worldwide selection is equally educational. Meals at **The Dining Room** at Kendall College let you brag about knowing future Michelin-starred chefs before they've made it big. As one of Chicago's premier culinary institutions, this college gives its chef trainees real-world guidance by way of elegant lunch and dinner service (reservations are required). Classes at Cooking Fools let home cooks hone their knife skills or prepare tamales from scratch, but if flaunting your newfound culinary credentials, swing by the **Wicker Park & Bucktown Farmer's Market**, before perusing **Olivia's Market** for specialty items, as well as a massive wine and beer selection.

BUCKTOWN & WICKER PARK

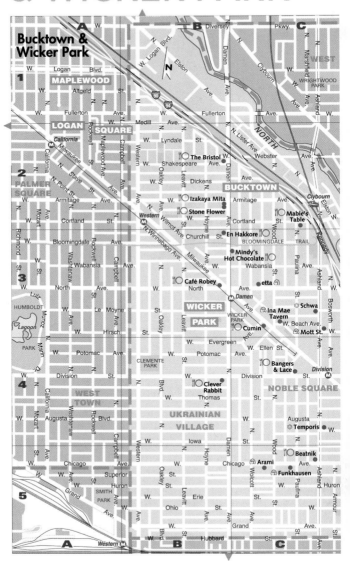

Bucktown & Wicker Park

MAPLEWOOD

LOGAN SQUARE

PALMER SQUARE

BUCKTOWN

WICKER PARK

HUMBOLDT PARK

WEST TOWN

UKRAINIAN VILLAGE

CLEMENTE PARK

NOBLE SQUARE

SMITH PARK

WEST WRIGHTWOOD PARK

BLOOMINGDALE TRAIL

The Bristol

Izakaya Mita

Stone Flower

Mable's Table

En Hakkore

Mindy's Hot Chocolate

Café Robey

etta

Schwa

Ina Mae Tavern

Cumin

Mott St.

Bangers & Lace

Clever Rabbit

Temporis

Beatnik

Arami

Funkhausen

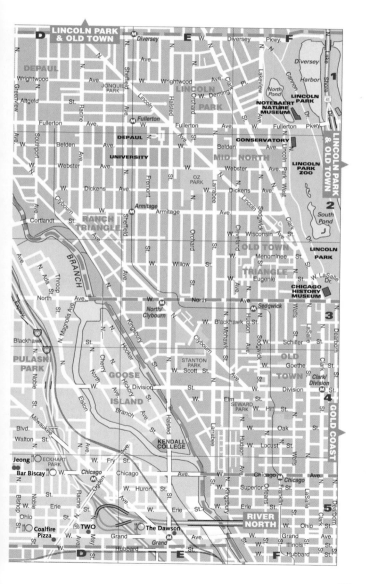

ARAMI ⓐ

Japanese • Contemporary Décor

🍶 ♿ 🍴   **MAP:** C5

Come to this bamboo-clad izakaya, with its comfortable sushi bar and soaring skylights, for impressively rendered small plates and specialty cocktails featuring Japanese spirits. The night's tsukemono can reveal spicy okra, crisp hearts of palm and sweet burdock root. The nigiri selection might showcase New Zealand King salmon topped with pickled wasabi root. The robata produces grilled maitakes with Japanese sea salt and black garlic purée; and gani korroke, a crunchy, creamy crab croquette, is plated with togarashi-spiked mayonnaise.

Don't turn down the all-ice cream dessert menu, which includes enticing flavors like coconut-cinnamon-banana. It comes nestled in granola-like bits of miso-graham cracker crumble for a finish as sweet as it is unique.

▦ 1829 W. Chicago Ave. (bet. Wolcott Ave & Wood St.)
🚇 Division
✆ (312) 243-1535 — **WEB:** www.aramichicago.com
▦ Closed Monday, Tuesday - Sunday lunch   **PRICE:** $$

BANGERS & LACE 🍴

Gastropub • Tavern

🍺 ♿ 🍴   **MAP:** C4

Despite the frilly connotations, this sausage-and-beer mecca's name refers not to doilies, but to the delicate layers of foam that remain in the glass after your craft brew has been quaffed. You'll also have plenty of opportunity to study the lace curtains as you plow through their extensive draft beer menu, noted on blackboards in the comfortably worn-in front bar room.

Decadent foie gras corn dogs (actually French garlic sausage wrapped with soft-sweet brioche cornbread) and veal brats with melted Gouda elevate the humble sausage; while a slew of sandwiches suit simpler tastes. Grilled cheese gilds the lily with taleggio, raclette, and Irish cheddar; and house-made chips drizzled with truffle oil and malt vinegar are more than a bar snack.

▦ 1670 W. Division St. (at Paulina St.)
🚇 Damen (Blue)
✆ (773) 252-6499 — **WEB:** www.bangersandlacechicago.com
▦ Closed Monday - Friday lunch   **PRICE:** $$

BAR BISCAY ¶O

Basque · Trendy

&

MAP: D5

This bright and beautiful addition to the Noble Square scene arrived courtesy of the team behind the popular mfk. Inside, the music can get loud, and the crowd even louder, but the bright lights and upbeat vibe is contagious, so have a few glasses of that vermouth (on tap!) and lean into it. You've landed at one of the trendiest places in town.

The dinner menu is laid out in groups like "from vegetables" or "from the sea. " The latter might unveil classic Basque dishes like a conserva of anchovies tossed with fennel, red onion and excellent olive oil; or even chewy razor clams bathed with a rich, herbaceous and lemony sauce. For dessert, a gargantuan strawberry crêpe tucked with quince and lemon-Neufchatel, has sweet addicts rightfully swooning.

■ 1450 W. Chicago Ave. (bet. Bishop St. & Greenview Ave.)
▣ Chicago (Blue)
℘ (312) 455-8900 — **WEB:** www.barbiscay.com
■ Closed lunch daily   **PRICE: $$**

BEATNIK ¶O

Fusion · Design

🍸 🏛 🍺 🚲

MAP: C5

Marked by a vast space, this is one of the more unique concepts to arrive on Chicago's culinary scene in recent times. Beatnik is nothing less than a sensory haven; amid all the bodies under glittering chandeliers, find double-height ceilings, repurposed street lights, an atrium, and colorful tiles—all of which evoke an inviting Mediterranean vibe.

Allow your gaze to wander away from the mesmerizing décor to focus on its diverse cuisine, infused with North African elements. Start with halloumi and fattoush, before savoring Cornish game hen tagine with cauliflower and turmeric purée. Sweetbread kebabs with vadouvan and zhoug speak to the team's versatility. Not everything is perfect, but there is talent here and joy to be had from Chef Marcos Campos' menu.

■ 1604 W. Chicago Ave. (at Ashland Ave.)
▣ Chicago (Blue)
℘ (312) 929-4945 — **WEB:** www.beatnikchicago.com
■ Closed Monday, Tuesday - Friday lunch   **PRICE: $$$**

THE BRISTOL ¶○

American • Neighborhood

MAP: B2

Get to know your neighbors a little better at this dim, bustling haunt boasting seasonal American fare with a Mediterranean twist. Regulars sit elbow-to-elbow at the concrete bar, squinting under filament bulbs to see the constantly changing menu's latest additions on chalkboards throughout the room.

Start with a Moscow Mule in a frosty copper mug to go with head-on prawns a la plancha with anchovy butter, or smoked whitefish dip with horseradish and saltines. Large plates sing with comfort, like the smoked pork tostada with adobo, tomatillo salsa, refried beans, and Chihuahua cheese. Like their drinks selection, brunch is a big hit and may include a hangover-curing noodle bowl or sweet cinnamon rolls. Homemade nutter butters make an indulgent finale.

- 2152 N. Damen Ave. (bet. Shakespeare & Webster Aves.)
- Western (Blue)
- (773) 862-5555 — **WEB:** www.thebristolchicago.com
- Closed Monday - Friday lunch   **PRICE: $$**

CAFÉ ROBEY ¶○

American • Chic

MAP: B3

Resting on one of the intersections of Chicago's famous six corners in Wicker Park, this stunning restaurant is nestled at the base of the chic Robey hotel. The room dazzles at every turn with its midcentury modern-meets-contemporary brasserie vibe, just as the kitchen turns out elegant reinterpretations of familiar dishes. Imagine the likes of butter-poached shrimp over tender escarole, or cod topped with a soft brioche, leek crust and sided by artichoke barigoule as well as crisp prosciutto ribbons. The terrific rhubarb clafoutis with a ginger-rhubarb sorbet is so good you won't want it to ever end. Brunch is available daily, so you'll no longer need to wait for the weekend.

Street views charm, but head to the rooftop for an even better vantage point.

- 1616 N. Milwaukee Ave. (at North Ave.)
- Damen (Blue)
- (872) 315-3084 — **WEB:** www.caferobey.com
- Open lunch & dinner daily   **PRICE: $$$**

CLEVER RABBIT ΨΟ

American • Contemporary Décor

MAP: B4

On a crowded stretch of Division, Clever Rabbit pulls away from the pack thanks to its inventive menu and rustic-chic space, featuring a marble-topped bar, whitewashed brick walls and modern lighting. The professional staff is well versed on the vegetable-forward menu, so heed their counsel and begin with the mushroom and polenta terrine with walnuts and a pumpkin marmalade. Then dive into carrot dumplings or the pig ear (shaped) pasta with braised broccoli rabe and ricotta. Finesse and flavor reign in such items as the North African chicken seasoned with ras el hanout or tuna with compressed cucumber and puffed wild rice.

Go ahead and dangle that carrot cake. This triple-layer treat with a cream cheese filling and olive oil "jam" is the ultimate reward.

- 2015 W. Division St. (bet. Hoyne & Damen Aves.)
- Division (Blue)
- (773) 697-8711 — WEB: www.cleverrabbitchicago.com
- Closed Monday - Friday lunch

PRICE: $$$

COALFIRE PIZZA ΨΟ

Pizza • Family

MAP: D5

Sure, you could come for a salad, but the focus here is on pizza—and yours should be, too. The dining room is cozy, showcasing an open kitchen where pie production is on full display for all to see. And in a playful bit of recycling, empty tomato sauce cans placed on each table become stands for sizzling pizzas churned straight from the 800-degree coal-fired oven.

This hot spot has its ratio down to a fine art and knows not to burden its thin and crispy crust that's blackened and blistered in all the right places. The mortadella is a delight, with chopped garlic and gossamer slices of peppercorn-flecked sausage. But if you wish to go your own way, build the perfect pie with toppings that run the gamut from decadent Gorgonzola to tangy goat cheese.

- 1321 W. Grand Ave. (bet. Ada & Elizabeth Sts.)
- Chicago (Blue)
- (312) 226-2625 — WEB: www.coalfirechicago.com
- Closed Monday, Tuesday - Thursday lunch

PRICE: $

CUMIN ¶O
Indian • *Neighborhood*

&

MAP: C3

Located on the main drag of Milwaukee Avenue, this cozy spot showcases its Nepali heritage and knowledge of Indian specialties via its cooking. While fans of the sub-continent love Cumin for its clean, modern surrounds, linen-lined tables struggle to contain the myriad plates that pile up during the lunchtime buffet.

Paintings of mountain scenes decorate crimson-red walls and prep diners for flavorful food from the Himalayan frontier. This menu has most of the usual suspects, but get gnawing on chicken momos (dumplings) accompanied by a tomato dipping sauce laced with turmeric, garlic, and chili powder. Soak up pieces of garlic naan in an intensely spiced lamb vindaloo stocked with soft potatoes. Cool down over a light and refreshing Taj Mahal lager.

- 1414 N. Milwaukee Ave. (bet. Evergreen & Wolcott Aves.)
- Damen (Blue)
- (773) 342-1414 — **WEB:** www.cumin-chicago.com
- Closed Monday lunch

PRICE: $

THE DAWSON ¶O
Gastropub • *Contemporary Décor*

MAP: E5

On cold nights, gathering around one of the fireplaces at this River West favorite hits all the right notes. The Dawson has everything you can ask for in a gastropub—a convivial vibe, clever bites and wraparound bar pouring stirring libations. Speaking of which, the Surfer Rosa with tequila, blood orange, and chilies, attracts spirited guests like moths to a flame. A communal table and open kitchen with counter offer multiple opportunities for meeting, greeting, and eating.

When hunger strikes, get nibbling on chicken fried lobster with spicy ranch or roasted cauliflower with a boldly spiced masala. Lest you forget, seared duck breast and sausage with Oaxacan mole is great for sharing; while a Bourbon caramel blondie sundae is the stuff of dessert dreams.

- 730 W. Grand Ave. (at Halsted St.)
- Grand (Blue)
- (312) 243-8955 — **WEB:** www.the-dawson.com
- Closed Monday - Friday lunch

PRICE: $$

EN HAKKORE 🍴

Korean · Simple

MAP: B3

Healthy doesn't have to be humdrum. This simple little Korean eatery, run by a husband-and-wife team and decorated with more than a hint of whimsy, specializes in big bowls of bibimbap. You choose your rice and protein, be it pork or barbecue beef, decide on the heat level and then dive straight in—up to 16 different vegetables are used and they're as tasty as they are colorful. Also worth trying are the steamed mandoo (pork dumplings) and the curiously addictive tacos made with paratha.

Simply place your order at the counter, grab a plastic fork and, if you're with friends, commandeer the large communal table. There's no alcohol (and it's not BYOB) so instead take advantage of an invigorating soft drink from the fridge. You'll feel so virtuous.

◻ 1840 N. Damen Ave. (bet. Churchill & Moffat Sts.)
◻ Damen (Blue)
✆ (773) 772-9880
◻ Closed Sunday

PRICE: $

ETTA 😀

American · Trendy

MAP: C3

Chef Danny Grant is at it again as he brings his distinctive flair and flavors to this live-fire hot spot. Inside, the space is less about glitz and more about a natural, lush and polished vibe. Lofty windows ensure the bi-level arena is flooded with light, but most of the action is centered around that open-flame kitchen.

Informed and pleasant servers steer diners through a panoply of inspired dishes, like complex salads, warming pastas, and wood-fired pizzas. The deliciously affordable "Pig Picnic" is a must among groups, while octopus panzanella with charred avocado and farfalle pomodoro with creamy burrata are beloved, individually sized bites. Mille crêpe with poached pear, oat streusel, and Earl Grey sorbet is an ingenious take on the classic treat.

◻ 1840 W. North Ave. (bet. Wolcott & Wood Sts.)
◻ Damen (Blue)
✆ (312) 757-4444 — **WEB:** www.ettarestaurant.com
◻ Closed Monday - Friday lunch

PRICE: $$

FUNKENHAUSEN 😊

Gastropub • Contemporary Décor

🍸 🍱 ♿ 🏛 🚠   **MAP:** C5

Don't let the name fool you. This isn't a lederhosen-wearing, beer stein-waving sort of spot. Instead, imagine a former warehouse-turned-chic setting for German-rooted, Southern-slanted food. The fact this is complemented by an ace beer selection, Bavarian-inspired cocktails, and wine list worth a deeper look simply adds to the allure.

Begin with garlic pretzel knots, served with mustard sauce and a pimento cheese dip for that signature Southern departure from German tradition. House-cured ham with smoked trout aïoli is tender to the point of creamy; pork sausage has that satisfying snap; and French onion spaetzel, in a caramelized onion béchamel, is utterly creative. Delicately charred pork chop set atop sauerkraut is a feast fit for more than one.

◼ 1709 W. Chicago Ave. (bet. Paulina & Wood Sts.)
🚇 Chicago (Blue)
📞 (312) 929-4727 — **WEB:** www.funkenhousen.com
◼ Closed Monday - Friday lunch   **PRICE:** $$

INA MAE TAVERN 😊

Creole • Rustic

🍸 ♿ 🚠   **MAP:** C3

Straddling a bustling corner, this handsome New Orleans-style tavern feels right at home in vibrant Wicker Park. The interior is stylish and vast, with a humming bar up front where patrons line up three-deep behind stools. Beyond that, find a casual dining space buzzing with an amiable, but professional staff.

Named for Executive Chef Brian Jupiter's great-grandmother, Ina Mae, the menu ticks off many NOLA classics. Think packed seafood po' boys and steaming gumbos, like the utterly delicious Ya-Ya, bobbing with shrimp, crawfish, chicken, and okra; or the pitch-perfect buttermilk-brined fried chicken, paired with pancakes, apple butter, and a side boat of gravy. The pineapple and coconut bread pudding soaked in rum will have sweet fans back in no time.

◼ 1415 N. Wood St. (at Beach Ave.)
📞 (773) 360-8320 — **WEB:** www.inamaetavern.com
◼ Closed Monday - Friday lunch   **PRICE:** $$

IZAKAYA MITA 🍴

Japanese • Simple

MAP: B2

This Bucktown favorite is a family-run tavern worth seeking out for its homespun take on izakaya eats and gracious hospitality.

Start with single-serve sake in a jar so cute you'll want to smuggle it home, or a cocktail inspired by Japanese literature (the Norwegian Wood, a delicious interpretation of the Haruki Murakami novel blends whiskey, Luxardo, sweet vermouth and orange bitters). The array of small plates brims with creativity and flavor: tsukune are coarse-ground, delightfully chewy and achieve a mouthwateringly charred exterior from having been grilled over binchotan; while tako-yaki are as delicious as any found on a Tokyo street cart. Korokke, a panko-crusted potato croquette, comes with tonkatsu sauce for delicious dunking.

- 1960 N. Damen Ave. (at Armitage Ave.)
- Western (Blue)
- (773) 799-8677 — **WEB:** www.izakayamita.com
- Closed Monday - Friday lunch

PRICE: $

JEONG 🍴

Korean • Contemporary Décor

MAP: D5

This sleek operation arrives courtesy of two passionate young chefs, Dave Park and wife Jen Tran. In this kitchen, they aim to impart complex and authentic Korean flavors to a myriad of sophisticated diners. All this transpires in an elegant, intimate and ultra-modern setting—and the result is foodie date-night perfection.

Chef Dave Park spins gorgeous, high quality ingredients into incredibly inventive dishes, combining excellent products with a deft hand. A delicate disk of salmon tartare, for example, is topped with doenjang yuzu gastrique, miniature quenelles of crème fraiche, and crunchy rice crackers that are full of nutty flavor; while an earthy kimchi truffle emulsion is paired with an accurately cooked bavette of beef and sunchoke croquette.

- 1460 W. Chicago Ave. (at Greenview Ave.)
- Chicago (Blue)
- (312) 877-5016 — **WEB:** www.jeongchicago.com
- Closed Sunday - Monday, Tuesday - Saturday lunch

PRICE: $$$

MABLE'S TABLE 🍴

American • Neighborhood

🛖 ♿

It's Mother's Day every day at Mable's Table, where Chef/owner Anthony Reyes pays homage to his own mamá with a spectrum of classic comfort food. This "table" is big on the cozy factor—just one of the reasons you'll find everyone here, from couples and children to suits closing deals over meals.

The menu may be concise but dishes leave a lasting impression. Whitefish is prepared simply with a crispy pan-sear and finished with a light Meyer lemon-butter sauce. Then move on to the pièce de résistance—porchetta bollio loaded with juicy, roast pork full of layers of sweet fat, dill pickles and cheese. It is quite simply heaven on a roll, with a side of fries, natch. For a balanced feast, finish with a wonderfully tart slice of key lime pie.

◼ 1655 W. Cortland St. (bet. Paulina St. & Marshfield Ave.)

✆ (773) 904-7433 — **WEB:** www.mablestable.com

◼ Open lunch & dinner daily   **PRICE: $$**

MINDY'S HOT CHOCOLATE 🍴

American • Friendly

♿ ♿

Bucktown wouldn't be the same without this sweet spot run by pastry chef extraordinaire, Mindy Segal. Diners walk past decadent hot chocolate mix and cookies on display before hitting an industrial-chic space fitted with sleek dark wood, caramel-brown walls and chocolate-toned leather banquettes.

Decadent chocolate is the name of the game, though diners will also discover delicious savory items. Try the roasted tomato soup, garnished with green onion slivers; or the BLT with pesto-seasoned aïoli, heirloom tomato, avocado and thick, crispy maple-cayenne bacon. An affogato—a scoop of coffee-cocoa nib ice cream paired with the chef's namesake hot chocolate—makes for the perfect finale.

Get your fix outside Bucktown at the outpost in Revival Food Hall.

◼ 1747 N. Damen Ave. (bet. St. Paul Ave. & Willow St.)

🚇 Damen (Blue)

✆ (773) 489-1747 — **WEB:** www.hotchocolatechicago.com

◼ Closed Monday, Tuesday lunch   **PRICE: $$**

MOTT ST. 🐸

Fusion • Trendy

🍴 🎪 🥢

MAP: C3

Inside this stand-alone structure in booming Bucktown, find a chicken wire-caged pantry stocked with jars of red pepper, black vinegar, and other pungent edibles—all of which appear again in the food on your plate.

Offerings at this hip haven crisscross the globe. Chef Edward Kim has a vivid imagination and his cooking takes detours through delicious landscapes. Start with empanadas full of Oaxacan cheese, kimchi, and served with a chimichurri-crème fraîche. Then, calamari bokum is wok-fried with spicy gochujang, crisped potatoes, and topped with crushed peanuts, but for a soothing signature, opt for boat noodles in a beef shank broth with pickled serrano chiles, prik phon rua, and fried shallots. Do keep an eye out for the special Chinese New Year menu.

🔲 1401 N. Ashland Ave. (at Blackhawk St.)

🚇 Division

☏ (773) 687-9977 — **WEB:** www.mottstreetchicago.com

🔲 Closed Monday, Tuesday - Saturday lunch   **PRICE:** $$

STONE FLOWER 🍴

Contemporary • Elegant

MAP: B2

Barely six months into service and this ambitious, 12-seat counter is already off to an impressive start. Chef Jake Bickelhaupt is back behind the stoves and is the primary tour de force prepping, cooking, and plating an extensive tasting menu that pairs exceptional ingredients with thoughtfully composed sauces. The ideas are wholly his own and lean heavily on Japanese influences. Winning plates include poached sturgeon in caviar sauce topped with a weave of fried Yukon gold potato strings; while A5 Miyazaki Wagyu is seared three times over the binchotan before being set in an ethereal blend of soy sauce aged in Japanese whisky barrels.

Guests may bring their own wine, but the pairing option flaunts well-aged bottles from top-shelf producers.

🔲 1952 N. Damen Ave. (bet. Armitage & Homer Sts.)

🚇 Damen

☏ (773) 831-3535 — **WEB:** www.stoneflowerchicago.com

🔲 Closed Sunday - Tuesday, Wednesday - Saturday lunch

PRICE: $$$$

SCHWA ✿
Contemporary · Trendy

BYO⊃

MAP: C3

There comes a point when pared-down style jumps from being easy-to-miss and becomes hard-to-forget. When a utilitarian and self-consciously bare-bones interior becomes attractively modern and industrial. When a lack of any FOH staff makes the service seem playfully all-hands-on-deck. The explicit rap music in the background reflects the deeply talented chefs' ethos, going well beyond laissez-faire to reach the point of "we don't give a damn. " You probably won't either once you taste the food—not every dish works, but when it does, the result is sublime.

Chef de Cuisine Norman Fenton makes his mark on this menu by way of the inventive "Welcome to Schwa" dish, unveiling a spicy Bloody Mary-inspired drink and crisp, savory waffle. The latter is intended to accompany the highlight of the course, namely: two rows of vibrant purées that spell out the greeting in Morse code. Such technical trickery continues into a plate of homemade pappardelle, laced with beurre monté and paired with peas and uni bubbles; or poached foie gras, delicately laid over trumpet mushrooms and mango gel.

Aged Parmigiano Reggiano with caramelized banana, nori, and Manuka honey presents an enticing blend of sweet and savory.

▢ 1466 N. Ashland Ave. (at Le Moyne St.)
▢ Division
☏ (773) 252-1466 — **WEB:** www.schwarestaurant.com
▢ Closed Sunday, Monday - Saturday lunch   **PRICE: $$$$**

TEMPORIS ✿

Contemporary • Elegant

&

Though this veritable jewel box deserves to have its name trumpeted in the streets, it is the epitome of serenity, sophistication and subtlety. With fewer than two-dozen seats, the space feels intimate, as if the whole show has been crafted for your benefit. The kitchen team here at Temporis flaunts their supreme talent. Each dish is a personal expression of their passion, vision and a clear representation of their highly intellectualized approach to cooking.

Custom tables featuring hydroponic sprouts that become part of your meal can also be found cradling such delicacies as escargot with a fermented sour cherry tomato. This then sets you on a course where you'll be surprised and delighted at every turn. Salmon in an uni broth; capellini with lobster morsels; a paper-thin biscuit with cured Mangalitsa pork—it's a culinary show of one intoxicating dish after the next. Ruby-red venison in a Madeira reduction is the stuff of dreams and may be tailed by decadent foie gras ice cream.

A chocolate tart is poured, then solidifies around a passion fruit-filled globe for a particularly dramatic final bow.

◼ 933 N. Ashland Ave. (at Walton St.)
▣ Division
☏ (773) 697-4961 — **WEB:** www.temporischicago.com
◼ Closed Sunday - Monday, Tuesday - Saturday lunch

PRICE: $$$$

TWO

American • Neighborhood

TWO is an urban interpretation of a Midwest tavern that was set up by two owners, features second-hand furnishings, and has an address whose last digit is—you guessed it—the number two. Beyond the vintage Toledo scales, find a reclaimed wood-paneled space dressed with antique meat cleavers, quaint ceiling fans and large barn doors.

This is a perfect lead into the farm-to-fork cuisine being whipped up in the open kitchen (the banquette across from it affords the best view). Start with classic Southern pimento cheese served in a miniature Mason jar alongside freshly grilled bread. Elegant small plates include pan-seared and spice-dusted halibut with fava beans and oyster mushrooms. On the sweet front, homemade puppy chow is chilled, crisp and delicious.

- 1132 W. Grand Ave. (at May St.)
- Chicago (Blue)
- (312) 624-8363 — **WEB:** www.113two.com
- Closed Monday, Tuesday - Sunday lunch

PRICE: $$

Sunday brunch plans?
Look for the 🥢!

EATING IN...
CHINATOWN & SOUTH

The Great Chicago Fire spared many of the South Loop's buildings, making the architecture here some of the oldest in the city. Residential palaces like the Glessner House and Clark House are now open for tours, but walk along Prairie Avenue for a self-guided view of these marvelous mansions. Further north, former lofts on Printers Row have been converted into condos, hotels, and restaurants, as has the landmark Dearborn Station—the oldest train depot in Chicago.

The South Loop has the breakfast scene covered— quite literally—with dishes piled high at casual neighborhood spots. Sop up a "South of the Border Benny" or any number of egg favorites at this area's outpost of **Yolk**, located on the southern end of Grant Park.

If you're strolling through the Museum Campus for lunch, grab cash for a bite at **Kim & Carlo's Hot Dog Cart** between the Field Museum and Shedd Aquarium. Vegetarians relish their special veggie dog with all the Chicago toppings, while everyone gets a great skyline view from Grant Park.

That ornate and arched gate at Wentworth Avenue and Cermak Road welcomes everyone to one of the largest Chinatowns in America. This iconic structure is an apt symbol for the neighborhood, where the local population is still predominantly Chinese-American. Many of the restaurants here offer classic Chinese-American fare that is an amalgam of Sichuan and Cantonese cuisines, but for a homemade spread, stock up on all things authentic at **Chinatown Market**. Additional inspiration can be

found by perusing a cookbook or two from the Chinatown branch of Chicago's Public Library. Don't forget to swing by to drool over the range of sweets at **Chiu Quon Bakery**, where cakes and other cream- or custard-filled pastries lay in wait. Of course, it's not summer in Chicago without baseball, so pay homage to the perennial city pastime by watching the White Sox do their thing on Guaranteed Rate Field, or the "Monsters of the Midway" take the gridiron inside Soldier Field's formidable walls.

Museums and learning centers showcase the Windy City's heritage from all angles. Apart from the collection of historic buildings in Grant Park's Museum Campus, this neighborhood is also home to Willie Dixon's Blues Heaven Foundation, whose mission is to preserve its musical legacy. With swooping green roof ornaments, the Harold Washington Library Center is impossible to miss, but an equally worthy site is their glass-ceilinged winter garden hidden inside.

CHINATOWN & SOUTH

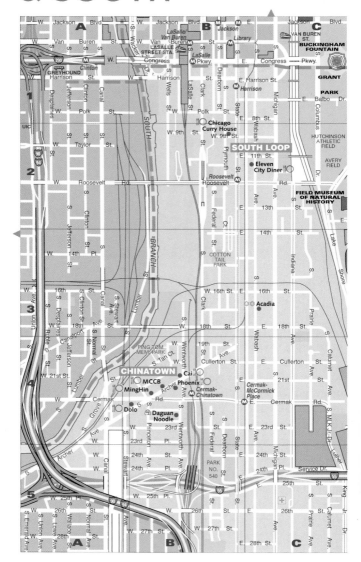

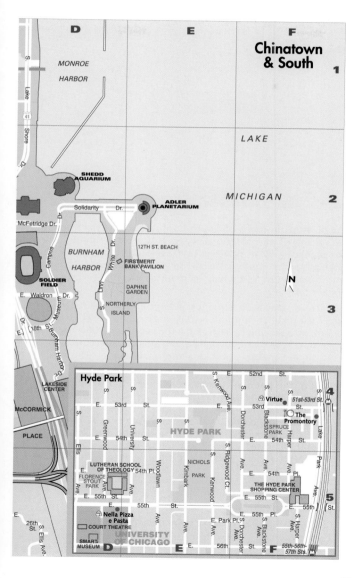

MONROE

HARBOR

LAKE

MICHIGAN

SHEDD
AQUARIUM

ADLER
PLANETARIUM

Solidarity   Dr.

2

McFetridge Dr.

BURNHAM

HARBOR

12TH ST. BEACH

FIRSTMERIT
BANK PAVILION

SOLDIER
FIELD

DAPHNE
GARDEN

E. Waldron   Dr.

N

NORTHERLY
ISLAND

3

18th

LAKESIDE
CENTER

Hyde Park

S. Kenwood Ave.

E.   52nd   St.

4

McCORMICK

S.   53rd   St.

E.   53rd   St.

S. Dorchester

Virtue   51st-53rd St.
53rd   St.

The
Promontory

PLACE

S.
Greenwood   Ave.

S.
University   Ave.

HYDE PARK

S. Blackstone
SPRUCE
PARK

S. Harper

Ellis

54th   St.

E.   54th   St.

S. Ridgewood Ct.

LUTHERAN SCHOOL
OF THEOLOGY 54th St.

NICHOLS
PARK

E.   54th   Pl.

E.
FLORENCE
STOUT
PARK

Woodlawn   Ave.

Kimbark   Ave.

S. Kenwood

THE HYDE PARK
SHOPPING CENTER

E.   55th   St.

E.   55th   St.

E.   55th   St.

E. 55th

(St.)

5

E.
26th
St.

S. Ellis Ave.

Nella Pizza
e Pasta

COURT THEATRE

SMART
MUSEUM

55th   St.

55th   Ave.

E. Park Pl.

E. 55th   Pl.

S. Dorchester
Ave.

S. Blackstone
Ave.

S. Harper Ave.

S. Harper   Ave.

Park   Ave.

Lake

UNIVERSITY
OF CHICAGO

D

E.   56th
E

55th-56th-
57th Sts.

F

ACADIA ✿✿
Contemporary · Luxury

🍸 ♿ 🍽 🦞

MAP: C3

One of the true gems of South Loop, Acadia is the impassioned restaurant of the talented Ryan McCaskey. Pulling from his Vietnamese heritage as well as his travels in Maine, Chef McCaskey's cooking is ambitious, precise and deliciously technical. Perhaps even more importantly, his kitchen's commitment to that vision is palpable in every bite.

Set between glassy apartment buildings and a small patch of grass, Acadia is a distinct stand-alone destination. The interior is decidedly elegant, with soaring ceilings and a soothing blend of warm neutrals, cool grays, as well as chocolate and sage peppered throughout the lofty space. Service is gracious and professional—the kind we all hope for but rarely find these days.

A guest at the bar can choose from an à la carte menu; while the dining room offers a seven-course feast. A meal in this brigade's sure hands might reveal an Isle au Haut scallop fresh off the coast of Maine, set over a raviolo filled with pastura con trufa cheese, ramps, morels and sumptuously finished with sauce Normande. The signature Yukon Gold potato "risotto" studded with tender leeks, sweet English peas, savory morels and truffle butter is pure excellence.

🔲 1639 S. Wabash Ave. (bet. 16th & 18th Sts.)
🚇 Cermak-Chinatown
📞 (312) 360-9500 — **WEB:** www.acadiachicago.com
🔲 Closed Monday - Tuesday, Wednesday - Sunday lunch

PRICE: $$$$

CAI

Chinese · Family

MAP: B4

It may be on the second floor of the Chinatown Mall, but a sleek carved wood and glass door marks the entrance to Cai, indicating that there is something special within. And indeed there is, as the place not only gleams but is packed with Chinese expats, families, and locals. They're all here for such spot-on Cantonese classics as barbecue pork, rice noodles, and congee. There's not a single cart in sight either, as dim sum is ferried to and fro by adept servers. Check off the box for such delicious nibbles as seafood dumplings in a flavorful broth; delicate xiao long bao with crab; or congee enriched by mushrooms. Set aside your table manners for a plate of their deliciously messy chicken feet.

Come during dinner for page-after-page of elegant entrées.

- 2100 S. Archer Ave. (at Wentworth Ave.)
- Cermak-Chinatown
- (312) 326-6888 — **WEB:** www.caichicago.com
- Open lunch & dinner daily

PRICE: $$

CHICAGO CURRY HOUSE

Indian · Family

MAP: B2

Maybe you sniff the wafting aromas of ginger, garlic, and cumin first; maybe you hear the sitar tinkling its welcoming notes as you enter. Either way, you know immediately that Chicago Curry House is a commendable showcase of Indian and Nepalese cuisines.

The lunchtime buffet lets you eat your fill with crispy papadum and baskets of naan; while dinner features an à la carte of faves including Nepalese khasi ko maasu, with bone-in goat bobbing in a velvety cardamom- and black pepper-sauce. Tandoori chicken is a smoky, moist delight; and butter chicken, creamy and rich in a tomato- and garam masala-spiced gravy, is done just right. The staff has helpful suggestions for dealing with the area's draconian parking restrictions; call ahead for tips.

- 899 S. Plymouth Ct. (at 9th St.)
- Harrison
- (312) 362-9999 — **WEB:** www.curryhouseonline.com
- Open lunch & dinner daily

PRICE: $

DAGUAN NOODLE 🤶
Chinese · Simple

 ♿   **MAP:** B4

Nonne have their minestrone, nanas have their chicken noodle soup, but for the best in comfort food Chinese-style, there's nothing better than these rice noodles in soup. The broth is prepared daily and whether you choose sour or spicy, or even the pig intestine and oxtail version, it tastes like liquid gold. Consuming this creation is great fun too, with a tray of vegetables and choice of protein—perhaps Chinese potted meats or flaky shrimp cake? Then, drop those bouncy rice noodles into the bubbling pot and wait for the magic to unfold. Regulars may round out this feast with such sumptuous sides as steamed pork buns, a cucumber salad or fluffy pumpkin pancakes.

The gleaming space is small but doesn't accept reservations (yet!), so expect a wait.

🔲 2230 S. Wentworth Ave. (bet. 23rd Pl. & 24th St.)
🚇 Cermak-Chinatown
📞 (312) 929-2758 — **WEB:** www.daguannoodle.com
🔲 Open lunch & dinner daily   **PRICE: $**

DOLO 🍴
Chinese · Contemporary Décor

 ♿   **MAP:** B4

Settled amidst the hustle and bustle of Archer Avenue is this rare and stylish gem. Dolo is welcoming and accessible, with a highly engaged service staff, full modern bar and plenty of on-site parking. And though it's a stone's throw from Cermak, it feels like a tucked-away treasure for locals in the know.

While there's delicious dim sum to be had, diners would do well to try their hand at the impressive specialty menu. Jellyfish is cut into tiny slivers and laced with a heavenly blend of chili oil and Sichuan peppercorns. Following this, steamed sea bass may be paired with pickled peppers, fragrant ginger, scallions and cilantro. For dinner, the tea-flavored chicken brined for two whole days, is the very essence of tenderness.

🔲 2222 S. Archer Ave. (bet. Princeton & Steward Aves.)
🚇 Cermak-Chinatown
📞 (312) 877-5117 — **WEB:** www.dolorestaurant.com
🔲 Open lunch & dinner daily   **PRICE: $$**

ELEVEN CITY DINER 🍴

Deli · Family

♿ � 🍽 🖥 🥂

MAP: C2

Nosh on a mile-high sandwich or chocolate malt at Eleven City Diner, a modern revival of the classic Jewish deli. Gleaming subway tiles play off retro leather booths and swiveling barstools, while jazz in the background keeps things moving with chutzpah and flair.

Diner standards include patty melts, sandwiches piled with corned beef or pastrami, knishes and latkes. Bubbe's chicken soup comes brimming with a fluffy matzo ball the size of a baseball; while Junior's cheesecake from Brooklyn or a triple-decker wedge of red velvet cake sates all the sweet-loving guests. A full-service deli counter offers salamis and smoked fish to-go. For a true blast from the past, stop by the candy stand near the entry, stocked with Bazooka Joe and other favorites.

■ 1112 S. Wabash Ave. (bet. 11th St. & Roosevelt Rd.)
🚇 Roosevelt
☎ (312) 212-1112 — **WEB:** www.elevencitydiner.com
■ Open lunch & dinner daily

PRICE: $

MCCB 🍴

Chinese · Contemporary Décor

♿ 🍽

MAP: B4

Modern Chinese Cookbook is the explanation behind the acronym of this modern retreat, tucked inside the sprawling Chinatown Square. You'll understand the name once you catch sight of their menu—it's a bible brimming with delicious selections leaning toward spicy Sichuan flavors.

Meat or fish cooked over applewood charcoal originated as a street food in Chongqing. But here it's one of the more unique items, and may be tailed by the equal parts spicy and sour pickle- and fish-soup, which packs a wallop for such a wee bowl. Finally, this kitchen also turns out an excellent version of wok-fried rabbit with cumin, peppercorn and cilantro, but their salt and pepper shrimp can't be skipped. Full of flavor with a brittle shell, these beauties are hard to resist.

■ 2138 S. Archer Ave. (in Chinatown Sq.)
🚇 Cermak-Chinatown
☎ (312) 881-0168 — **WEB:** www.mccbchicago.com
■ Open lunch & dinner daily

PRICE: $$

MINGHIN ❗️○
Chinese • Chic

♿ ⟳ 🖥 🥢   **MAP:** B4

Conveniently situated on the ground level of Chinatown Square, MingHin is a stylish standby that draws a diverse crowd to the neighborhood. Spacious dining rooms separated by wooden lattice panels offer seating for a number of occasions, from casual booths and large banquet-style rounds to specially outfitted tables for hot pots.

Dim sum is a popular choice even on weekdays, with diners making selections from photographic menus rather than waiting for a passing cart. Among the numerous options, juicy har gow, stuffed with plump seasoned shrimp, always hits the spot. Pan-fried turnip cakes are simultaneously crispy and creamy, studded with bits of pork and mushroom. Fluffy and subtly sweet Malay steamed egg cake is a rare find for dessert.

🟦 2168 S. Archer Ave. (at Princeton Ave.)
🚇 Cermak-Chinatown
☎ (312) 808-1999 — **WEB:** www.minghincuisine.com
🟦 Open lunch & dinner daily   **PRICE: $$**

NELLA PIZZA E PASTA 😀
Italian • Contemporary Décor

♿ 🏯   **MAP:** D5

The name of this delicious Hyde Park offering belongs to chef and owner, Nella Grassano, a classically trained pizzaiola. Together with her restaurateur partner, Francesco, the couple's warm hospitality is the icing on the cake to an experience built around solid cooking. Favorite items include house-made pasta, laced with pristine ingredients and cooked to al dente perfection; or blistered Neapolitan pies, so fresh and authentic they'll transport you straight to the Italian countryside.

Don't sleep on the starters though, like calamari affogati braised to perfection in a spicy tomato sauce studded with salt-brined black olives. Sop up the incredible sauce with Grassano's lip-smacking bread, baked in-house and served warm from the wood-burning oven.

🟦 1125 E. 55th St. (at University Ave.)
☎ (773) 643-0603 — **WEB:** www.nellachicago.com
🟦 Open lunch & dinner daily   **PRICE: $$**

PHOENIX 🍴

Chinese • Family

MAP: B4

Dim sum lovers get the best of both worlds at Phoenix, a comfortable room that boasts a grand view of the Chicago skyline. Here, stacks of bamboo baskets are wheeled to tables on signature silver trolleys for a classic experience—yet each diner's selection is cooked to order for fresh and steaming-hot bites. The proof is in the soft and poppable shrimp-and-chive dumplings and the fluffy white buns stuffed with chunks of barbecue pork.

Those looking for larger portions will appreciate the meandering menu, which also boasts Hong Kong-style stir-fry and clay pot dishes alongside Americanized Chinese classics. Steamed sea bass fillets swim in soy oil on an oval platter and are sprinkled with a touch of slivered scallion to brighten the delicately flaky fish.

2131 S. Archer Ave. (bet. Princeton & Wentworth Aves.)
Cermak-Chinatown
(312) 328-0848 — **WEB:** www.chinatownphoenix.com
Open lunch & dinner daily

PRICE: $$

THE PROMONTORY 🍴

American • Trendy

MAP: F4

The Promontory has brought a bright and bustling gathering place to the Hyde Park community and you'll easily lose track of time while listening to the DJ-curated groovy tunes. Under lofty ceilings trimmed with black iron beams and sleek wood accents, urbanites sip hand-crafted cocktails around a central bar.

A white-hot fire blazes away in the open kitchen, providing the "hearth to table" food trumpeted on the menu. Banish bad memories of soggy lunch boxes and go for the fried bologna sandwich, with thick slices of house-cured bologna crisped on the griddle, then paired with tart sauerkraut, melted Swiss cheese and folded into marble rye. Banana-nut bread with whipped cream, caramelized banana slices and loads of syrup makes for a nice dessert.

5311 S. Lake Park Ave. (bet. 53rd & 54th Sts.)
(312) 801-2100 — **WEB:** www.promontorychicago.com
Open lunch & dinner daily

PRICE: $$

VIRTUE

Southern • Contemporary Décor

MAP: F4

Occupying a corner of Hyde Park within view of the University of Chicago, this is an inviting retreat with a welcoming bar, striking dining room, and buzzy kitchen helmed by the very talented Erick Williams. His well-executed Southern cooking draws a smart crowd, largely from the university nearby.

For starters, imagine skillet corn bread with a steak knife for slicing and slathering on the honey butter, while dirty rice topped with chicken gizzards is just what the soul ordered. Don't miss the butcher's snack, a selection of house-made charcuterie with pepper jelly. Southerners seek out the Geechie Boy grits with white cheddar for a stone-ground taste of home, but ganache-filled chocolate cake with Bourbon cherries will have dessert fans back in no time.

- 1462 E. 53rd St. (at Harper Ave.)
- (773) 947-8831 — **WEB:** www.virtuerestaurant.com
- Closed Monday - Tuesday, Wednesday - Friday lunch

PRICE: $$

Share the journey with us!
@MichelinGuideCH
@MichelinInspectors

EATING IN...
GOLD COAST

The Gold Coast is one of Chicago's poshest neighborhoods, flaunting everything from swanky high-rises on Lake Shore Drive to dazzling boutiques dotting Michigan Avenue. Its architecture is as stunning as its designer clothing. Here, find mansions crafted in regal Queen Anne, Georgian Revival, or Richardsonian Romanesque styles. However, this neighborhood is not all about the glitz; it is also deeply committed to the arts as a whole, housing both the Museum of Contemporary Art and the world-leading Newberry Library. Culture vultures are sure to uncover something edgy and unique at A Red Orchid Theater, after which the exotic Indian lunchtime buffet at **Gaylord** steals the show. Locals also knows how to party here. Visit any nightclub, pub, or restaurant along Rush and Division, stay out until dawn, and find breakfast on the burner at **The Original Pancake House**. Can there be anything better than fluffy pancakes and towering waffles after a late night?

They say breakfast is the most important meal, and at **The Lunchroom**, it's possible to start the day off right with their build-your-own breakfast menu and terrific to-go options. There is also some darn good junk food to be had in this white-gloved capital of chic. American comfort classics like sliders, burgers, and mac and cheese find their way into the carte at **LuxBar**, a dynamic lounge with some of the best people-watching in town. At lunch, **Gold Coast Dogs** packs them in for deliciously charred dogs, topped with gooey cheddar. Otherwise, simply humor your hot dog hankering by joining the constant queue outside **Downtown Dogs**.

Craving a bit of sweet? Make your way to **Corner Bakery Café** for a fleet of bakery-fresh treats—their signature golden-brown cinnamon crème cake has been drawing residents for over two decades now. **Tea Gschwendner** is where to go to lose yourself in a world of exotic selections. And, if you don't feel like steeping your own "Sencha Claus" blend, then snag a seat at **Argo Tea** where clouds of whipped cream and flavorful iced drinks are all part of the fun. Of course, this is the Gold Coast, so dress up for a proper afternoon cuppa at **The Drake's Palm Court**. Also housed in The Drake is warm and luxurious **Coq d'Or**, famous for its spectrum of classic cocktails, comfort food specials, and live weekend entertainment. Finally, over on Delaware Place, impeccable wines along with specialty cocktails aren't the only things heating up the scene at **Drumbar**—this rooftop scene at the Raffaello Hotel also lets fashionable crowds frolic alfresco at all hours of the night.

GOLD COAST

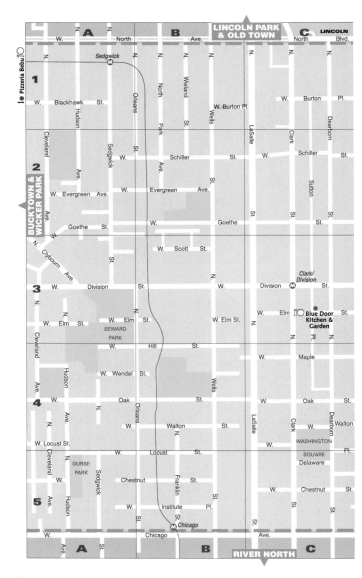

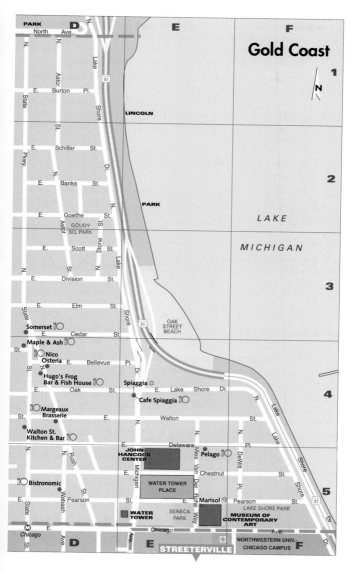

Gold Coast

N

PARK
North Ave.

E. Burton Pl.

State

Astor

Lake

Shore

Dr.

41

LINCOLN

St.

E. Schiller St.

Pkwy.

N.

E. Banks St.

E. Goethe St.

Astor

GOUDY
SQ. PARK

St.

E. Scott St.

PARK

Lake

Shore

Dr.

N.

E. Division St.

E. Elm St.

State

St.

Somerset 🍴⭕

E. Cedar St.

Maple & Ash 🍴⭕

St.

🍴⭕ Nico
Osteria

E. Bellevue Pl.

St.

Hugo's Frog
Bar & Fish House 🍴⭕

Spiaggia ❀

Dr.

E. Oak St.

E. Lake Shore Dr.

Cafe Spiaggia 🍴⭕

N.

🍴⭕ Margeaux
Brasserie

St.

E. Walton

Walton St.
Kitchen & Bar 🍴⭕

N.

St.

N.

E. Delaware Pl.

DeWitt

Lake

🍴⭕ Bistronomic

Rush

St.

JOHN
HANCOCK
CENTER

E. Michigan

Mies Van Der Rohe Way

Pelago 🍴⭕

E. Chestnut St.

Shore

Wabash

E. Pearson St.

WATER TOWER
PLACE

St.

Marisol 🏠

Pearson

LAKE SHORE PARK

Dr.

41

State

Ave.

WATER
TOWER

SENECA
PARK

MUSEUM OF
CONTEMPORARY
ART

M

E.

Chicago

St.

Ave.

Chicago

Ave.

NORTHWESTERN UNIV.-
CHICAGO CAMPUS

**LAKE
MICHIGAN**

OAK
STREET
BEACH

D   **E**   **F**

STREETERVILLE

1

2

3

4

5

BISTRONOMIC 🍴

French • Bistro

♿ 🚻 ⏰ 🛋 🎽   **MAP:** D5

Tucked away from the buzz of the Magnificent Mile, Bistronomic is a great place to cool your tired heels. Jaunty red awnings beckon brightly, and the revolving door spins guests into a warm room that's focused on the bonhomie of dining with friends. Oxblood walls, gray banquettes and a central bar play up the bistro feel, while the kitchen conveys creativity with fresh renditions of tasty classics.

Rusticity and elegance come together in a fillet of Lake Superior whitefish that is pan-seared to golden-brown and matched with spring ratatouille, preserved lemon and puréed eggplant. Exquisitely crisp feuilletine is a glamorous upgrade to the classic Kit Kat bar, folded with hazelnuts, bittersweet chocolate and finished with a sweet-tart orange sauce.

🔲 840 N. Wabash Ave. (bet. Chestnut & Pearson Sts.)
🚇 Chicago (Red)
📞 (312) 944-8400 — **WEB:** www.bistronomic.net
🔲 Closed Monday - Tuesday lunch   **PRICE: $$**

BLUE DOOR KITCHEN & GARDEN 🍴

American • Elegant

🚻 ⏰ 🛋   **MAP:** C3

Thank chef-to-the-stars Art Smith for raising the stakes of the local dining scene with this relaxed bistro.

In 1871, this carriage house home is said to have survived the Great Chicago Fire. Today, the cozy and well-appointed dining room makes the most of its parquet floors, Louis XV-style chairs, welcoming bar, and open kitchen where Southern-leaning fare is prepared in full view. Deviled eggs are a solid staple, elevated ever so slightly with pickled peppers, and the juicy, crunchy fried chicken is a hit for a reason. Signature desserts, like the towering slice of hummingbird cake layered with banana and pineapple or the scrumptious bread pudding, are sized to share. This place becomes even more charming when the weather warms and the patio opens.

🔲 52 W. Elm St. (bet. Clark & Dearborn Sts.)
🚇 Clark/Division
📞 (312) 573-4000 — **WEB:** www.bluedoorkitchenchicago.com
🔲 Open lunch & dinner daily   **PRICE: $$**

CAFE SPIAGGIA 🍴

Italian · Chic

MAP: E4

Welcome to the less formal, more approachable, all-day extension of Tony Mantuano's grande-dame Spiaggia, which is located just next door. The setting of this café is relaxed yet stylish; and dining here is a great way to enjoy unforgettable lakeside views for a fraction of the cost as its older sibling.

Expect a casual menu of simple lunchtime bites and sandwiches that gives way to a more composed yet still appetizing offering at dinner. But regardless of when you visit, house-made pastas are a particular highlight, especially those short tubes of lumache bathed with a rich and rustic lamb ragù. Don't miss out on generous portions of their fun and creative desserts, like pizzelle cookies sandwiching toasted milk gelato with chocolate-hazelnut crunch.

980 N. Michigan Ave. (at Oak St.)

Chicago (Red)

(312) 280-2750 — **WEB:** www.spiaggiarestaurant.com/cafe

Closed Sunday lunch

PRICE: $$

HUGO'S FROG BAR & FISH HOUSE 🍴

American · Trendy

MAP: D4

Housed in a sprawling setting adjacent to big brother Gibson's, Hugo's always seems packed. The vast dining room sets white linen-topped tables amid dark polished wood and pale walls decorated with a mounted swordfish, fish prints, and model ships. Hugo's bar draws its own crowd with abundant counter seating. The menu focuses on a selection of fish, steaks, and chops, supplemented by stone crab claws, oysters, crab cakes, chowders, and sautéed frog's legs. Family-style sides—creamed spinach or roasted Brussels sprouts in Bourbon maple butter—are a worthy addition.

With generous portions all around, you'll need a football team to share a slice of the Muddy Bottom Pie, or just a handful of pals to savor other decadent desserts like the apple pie.

1024 N. Rush St. (bet. Bellevue Pl. & Oak St.)

Clark/Division

(312) 640-0999 — **WEB:** www.hugosfrogbar.com

Closed lunch daily

PRICE: $$$

MAPLE & ASH 🍴

Steakhouse • Trendy

MAP: D4

Did someone say scene? Oh darling, that's half the fun at Chicago's buzziest steakhouse, Maple & Ash. Deep-set leather couches, clubby music and even a photo booth lend the multilevel marvel an irresistible party vibe.

This restaurant is set to the soft glow emanating from the semi-open kitchen, where a wood-fired hearth lights up dry-aged steakhouse classics, cut to generous proportions. Seafood lovers will find plenty to mull over too, like a tangle of octopus and squid, prepared in the wood-fueled oven and served with dill yogurt, arugula and roasted potatoes. Then, a fire-roasted seafood tower is brought tableside, featuring lobster tail, scallops, Manila clams and king crab, all bathed in garlic butter, chili oil and served with house-made pasta.

- 8 W. Maple St. (bet. Dearborn & State Sts.)
- Clark/Division
- (312) 944-8888 — **WEB:** www.mapleandash.com
- Closed Monday - Saturday lunch   **PRICE: $$$$**

MARGEAUX BRASSERIE 🍴

French • Elegant

MAP: D4

Margeaux Brasserie is one swank spot. Housed inside the Waldorf Astoria, this restaurant marks the first Chicago venture for the popular Mina Group, led by esteemed San Francisco-based chef, Michael Mina. The space is bright and airy, with light streaming in through the large picture windows and lots of luxe velvet and leather details.

Kick things off with perfectly caramelized duck wings a' l'orange. Diners may then choose to linger over dishes like the warm tomato Tatin, paired with puff pastry, Camembert and pistou. While a bone-in rack of lamb takes satisfaction to the next level when coupled with stewed chickpeas, piquillos and fennel, turnip with roasted lamb jus and a croustillant filled with braised lamb rib is the very picture of decadence.

- 11 E. Walton St. (at Rush St.)
- Chicago (Red)
- (312) 625-1324 — **WEB:** www.michaelmina.net
- Open lunch & dinner daily   **PRICE: $$$**

MARISOL 👄
American • Contemporary Décor

♿ 🍽

MAP: E5

Despite its location in the Museum of Contemporary Art, Marisol is so much more than a museum food court. This restaurant takes its name from the late French pop art sculptor, whose work was the museum's first acquisition.

The local, seasonal, and sensible cooking appeals to all palates, though much of the menu focuses on vegetables. Start with the burrata, a ubiquitous dish ramped up here with blood orange segments, almond crumble, and vanilla oil. This kitchen grills a perfect steak sided by cauliflower in a bright and flavorful huckleberry vinaigrette. The earthy buttermilk rye cake is expertly balanced by creamy pumpkin mousse and a quenelle of Mexican hot chocolate ice cream.

Hit the Counter for coffee, pastries, and quick bites on the go.

▪ 205 E. Pearson St. (at Mies Van Der Rohe Way)
▪ Chicago (Red)
☏ (312) 799-3599 — **WEB:** www.marisolchicago.com
▪ Closed Monday, Sunday dinner

PRICE: $$

NICO OSTERIA 🍴
Italian • Contemporary Décor

♿ 🛖 🍷 🖥 🍽 🔥

MAP: D4

Buzzworthy and a hit since day one, Chef Paul Kahan's local darling is one of the most likeable restaurants in town. It's more trendsetting than trendy, and the accommodating staff ensures that no one leaves disappointed.

The carte focuses on Italian-leaning seafood dishes, with inspired crudo like hamachi with cara cara orange flesh and garlic chips, or tuna with grilled grapefruit and crispy kale. Take a counter seat at the open kitchen to see just how the Kindai tuna with black trumpet mushrooms and kumquat comes together. The regional menu may also highlight such boldly flavored oceanic treats as chili-cured swordfish with thin, house-made grissini. Desserts, especially the butterscotch cremoso, may be playful in plating, but serious in flavor.

▪ 1015 N. Rush St. (at Bellevue Pl.)
▪ Chicago (Red)
☏ (312) 994-7100 — **WEB:** www.nicoosteria.com
▪ Open lunch & dinner daily

PRICE: $$$

PELAGO 🍴

Italian • Elegant

♿ 🚻 ☂ 🍽   **MAP:** E5

This jewel box of a spot is fittingly set adjacent to the Raffaello Hotel. Oozing with elegance, it boasts a crisp style via large windows, tasteful artwork and comfortable leather seats. An azure-blue color theme ensures the mood is serene. If the décor doesn't evoke the Med, then the Italian-leaning dishes will do the trick. Baked lasagna layered with tender noodles, tomato sauce, béchamel and veal ragù is both delicate and satisfying. A rustic, pan-roasted pork chop cooked a-la-Nonna-style and sided by mashed potatoes is particularly comforting.

Some may swap dessert for cheese, but the spumoni, a frozen vanilla sabayon sliced into triangular wedges and topped with fresh strawberries, is a light, slightly-sweet, and elegant finish.

▪ 201 E. Delaware Pl. (at Mies van der Rohe Way)
▪ Chicago (Red)
✆ (312) 280-0700 — **WEB:** www.pelagorestaurant.com
▪ Open lunch & dinner daily   **PRICE: $$$**

PIZZERIA BEBU 👻

Pizza • Contemporary Décor

♿ 🚻 🛋   **MAP:** N/A

Chicago and pizza go together like peanut butter and jelly, but does the Windy City need yet another shop dedicated to the crusty stuff? If it is Pizzeria Bebu, you bet your brick-lined gas oven it does. This excellent rendition gives any of its kind a run for their money.

A crispy crust with cornicione that crackles with flavor—this is a first-class pizza. You can't go wrong here, whether you veer simple with a Margherita (San Marzano tomatoes and mozzarella); have a little fun (crumbled meatballs, giardiniera, ricotta cheese and parmesan); or go nutty with nutless pesto, vodka sauce and fresh mozzarella. Pizzas may be the star at this gleaming, modern restaurant, but the thick and fluffy frittata proves that their other staples deserve equal billing.

▪ 1521 N. Fremont St. (bet. Weed & Blackhawk Sts.)
▪ North/Clybourn
✆ (312) 280-6000 — **WEB:** www.bebu.pizza
▪ Closed Tuesday - Wednesday   **PRICE: $$**

SOMERSET 🍴

American • Design

MAP: D3

If the Great Gatsby himself opened a restaurant, it might look something like the unabashedly gorgeous Somerset, the Boka Restaurant Group's long-awaited sashay onto the Gold Coast dining scene. And what an arrival indeed—nestled within the stylish Viceroy hotel and featuring what can only be described as a sublime yacht-club décor, with gilded mirrors, curvy blue banquettes and luminous art deco light fixtures.

Chef Lee Wolen's seasonal American cuisine is beautifully executed and surprising in all the right ways. Don't miss the smoked beet tartare, elevated to such heights you might never go back to beef, or flawless squid ink chitarra. A deconstructed carrot cake, tucked with buckwheat tuille, cream cheese mousse and blood orange, is divine.

1112 N. State St. (bet Franklin & Wells Sts.)

Clark/Division

(312) 586-2150 — **WEB:** www.somersetchicago.com

Open lunch & dinner daily

PRICE: $$$

WALTON ST. KITCHEN & BAR 🍴

American • Elegant

MAP: D4

Housed at the base of a glamorous new condo complex, this upscale bistro features a beautifully appointed space—with an elegant staircase that leads you upstairs to an oversized, U-shaped bar with tufted leather booths along one wall. Service everywhere is thoughtful and practiced.

Diners can expect a wide range of refined comfort food, from a spinach and goat cheese salad with warm bacon vinaigrette to a Nordic twist on salmon tartare. The latter is laced with juniper, pickled shallots and topped with toasted triangles of marbled rye bread. Light but satisfying entrées include a well-charred grilled chicken over panzanella studded with cherry tomatoes and spring vegetables. Be sure to request the optional bread basket—it's heaven for carb fans.

912 N. State St. (bet. Delaware Pl. & Walton St.)

(773) 570-3525 — **WEB:** www.waltonstreetchicago.com

Closed Monday - Friday lunch

PRICE: $$

SPIAGGIA ✿
Italian · Elegant

MAP: E4

Located in the striking One Magnificent Mile building, there are many reasons why Spiaggia remains one of the city's most beloved Italian restaurants. There are high-end bells and whistles aplenty, but to hear the staff recite the effort and intricacies behind, say, the culurgiones is to compel you to order them.

Good-looking groups and cozy couples with a glass of wine in hand make up most of the crowd here. Bread is a noteworthy assortment, including a dark ash loaf with a crusty exterior begging to be smeared with honey-drizzled whipped ricotta. Mafaldine pasta is especially delectable with tender shredded lamb belly; while the salmon, in a fennel cream studded with salmon roe, will have you wishing for seconds. The rabarbaro dessert is a delicate cheesecake dressed with rhubarb sorbet. Of course, if the many tempting options prove too much, opt for the tasting menu, which delivers all of the highlights without any of the decision making.

All in all, to dine at Spiaggia is to celebrate a Chicago grande-dame. The stunning dining room is designed with marble columns and alcoves to enhance its dramatic views, thereby making it an idyllic spot to appreciate the Magnificent Mile by night.

■ 980 N. Michigan Ave. (at Oak St.)
🚇 Chicago (Red)
✆ (312) 280-2750 — **WEB:** www.spiaggiarestaurant.com
■ Closed lunch daily

PRICE: $$$$

EATING IN...
HUMBOLDT PARK & LOGAN SQUARE

A charming pair of lively North Side neighborhoods, Humboldt Park and Logan Square have long been revered as Chicago's heart and soul. Here, delightful eateries abound, including **Smalls**—a smoke hut with an Asian twist. Their hickory-smoked brisket on Texas toast with Thai-style "tiger cry" sauce has earned a cult following for good reason. **Joong Boo Market** flaunts delicacies from rice cakes and ground red pepper flakes to dried vegetables and seaweed snacks.

Stroll further along these tree-lined streets until you reach kid-friendly **Bang Bang Pie Shop**; then wander into **Global Garden**, a community venture where immigrants grow produce for sale at local farmers' markets or CSAs. Other like-minded operations include **Campbell Co-op** and **Drake Garden**. Humboldt Park is also home to a vibrant Puerto Rican community—the annual Puerto Rican Festival features four days of festivities, fun, and great food. For Latin treats, sojourn at **Café Colao** and sample a cheese-and-guava-pastelillo, while seafood rules the roost at Bill Dugan's **The Fishguy Market**. Also renting space in this area are **Wellfleet**, a popular luncheonette; **Dante's Pizzeria** serving rollicking pies; **Landbirds,** lauded for excellent chicken wings; and **Shokolad**, a Ukranian haunt for pastries, cheesecakes, and lollipops.

An eclectic mix of cuisines combined with historic landmarks attract all and sundry to this lovely quarter. Find a mix of home chefs, star cooks, and staunch foodies at **Kurowski's Sausage Shop**, a respected butcher specializing in handmade cuts of Polish meats. Pick up pickles to-go

from the old-school and always-reliable **Dill Pickle Food Co-op**. Then tuck into neighborhood cafe, **Cellar Door Provisions**, for a variety of freshly baked breads and European-style pastries. Snag a bottle or two at **Diversey Wines**, a highly curated wine shop that stocks top organic and biodynamic producers in the U.S. and Europe. **Gaslight Coffee Roasters** is a caffeine junkie's real-life fantasy. Kids delight in **Margie's Candies**, while adults revel in gin-infused cocktails at **Scofflaw** as well as at local cocktail legend, Paul McGee's **Lost Lake Tiki Bar**. Food wonks shop till they drop at **Independence Park Farmers' Market**. Less locally traditional but just as tantalizing is **Jimmy's Pizza Café**, rightfully mobbed for its mean rendition of a New York-style slice. Albany Park is yet another melting pot of global foods and gastronomic retreats—sans the sky-high prices. If meat is what you're craving, join the crowds at time-tested burger joint, **Charcoal Delights**.

HUMBOLDT PARK & LOGAN SQUARE

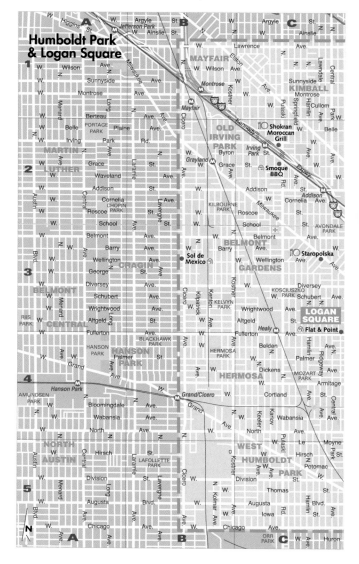

Humboldt Park & Logan Square

Shokran Moroccan Grill

Smoque BBQ

Sol de Mexico

Staropolska

Flat & Point

ARBOR ▮○

American • Simple

MAP: E3

Set in the historic-turned-hipster Green Exchange building, this is a coffee shop that also proffers a "Midwestern Omakase" on Friday and Saturday. Ingredients grown in the converted alley let the kitchen shine at all times. Concealed in grey curtains, the space exudes an air of mystery—not unlike the chefs themselves, who've earned the term "food and flavor nerds." And while there's much that's unusual here, when it comes to sustainability, awareness, and taste, this kitchen brings its A game. Dishes spin to the mood of Mother Nature, but expect such delights as pea soup with Belper Knolle goat cheese; or ham and eggs, starring black garlic soubise, chorizo, and a soft-cooked hen egg.

In lieu of dessert, delve into the thoughtful and quirky wine program.

▪ 2545 W. Diversey Ave. (bet. Maplewood Ave. & Rockwell St., in the Green Exchange Complex)

▪ California (Blue)

✆ (312) 866-0795 — **WEB:** www.arborprojects.com

▪ Closed Sunday, Monday - Thursday dinner, Saturday lunch

PRICE: $$$

BIXI BEER ▮○

Asian • Contemporary Décor

MAP: D3

Equal parts sophisticated Asian eatery and brewpub, BiXi has style to spare—with a glamorous, sun-soaked and plant-filled atrium of a dining room. Named for one of the nine sons of the Dragon King in Chinese mythology, its house brews often incorporate Eastern ingredients, like the dried mango and black tea that infuse a golden pale ale.

The menu is equally inventive, fusing Chinese and Chicago cuisines in creations like a Prime rib-stuffed bao with Sichuan-spiced giardiniera. The house-made Yibin-style belt noodles are equally irresistible, thanks to a generous helping of umami-rich fermented black beans. And for dessert, indulge in a mountain of coffee-cinnamon soft-serve accompanied by caramel and crispy puffed rice—it's big enough for four.

▪ 2515 N. Milwaukee Ave. (bet. Logan Blvd & Sacramento Ave.)

▪ Logan Square

✆ (773) 904-7368 — **WEB:** www.bixi.beer

▪ Open lunch & dinner daily

PRICE: $$

DAISIES
Italian • Neighborhood

MAP: D3

Kids, friends, neighbors—everyone seems to adore Daisies, and what's not to love? With its tiny, hardworking kitchen, clean, mid-century modern design and decidedly affordable prices, this local charmer can do no wrong.

Pastas reign supreme in this house, and there's even a smattering of gluten-free options. Other fun, delicious specialty dishes, like the house onion dip or fried mushrooms with cheese curds, show off the kitchen's playful side, along with more thoughtful creations like tajarin with chicken crackling, or mezzaluna stuffed with fermented squash and lamb. Veggie treats like braised leeks offer such intense flavor, you won't miss the meat. Finally, a thoughtful wine list celebrates domestic regions, including some from home state, Illinois.

2523 N. Milwaukee Ave. (bet. Logan Blvd. & Sacramento Ave.)
Logan Square
(773) 661-1671 — **WEB:** www.daisieschicago.com
Closed Monday - Tuesday, Wednesday - Saturday lunch

PRICE: $$

DOS URBAN CANTINA
Mexican • Contemporary Décor

MAP: D4

After several years at Topolobampo, the husband-wife duo behind this gem have taken their knowledge and skills to craft this consistently delicious and inventive cuisine. And, the chefs' deep understanding of Mexican ingredients has allowed them to create elegant and well-priced compositions. Chunks of slowly braised pork carnitas are hearty, tender and brought to an entirely new level with squash that pops with bright flavor—all balanced with a bracing tomatillo broth. For dessert, indulge in an excellent Mexican sugar pie topped with whipped cream and pecan toffee that is out of this world.

The space is comfortable and roomy, so that the steady stream of thirty-somethings never make it feel crowded. Curved booths and romantic lighting lend a warm vibe.

2829 W. Armitage Ave. (at Mozart St.)
California (Blue)
(773) 661-6452 — **WEB:** www.dosurbancantina.com
Closed Monday - Tuesday, Wednesday - Sunday lunch

PRICE: $$

FAT RICE 😊
Macanese • Trendy

 ♿ 🍸

MAP: D3

Not familiar with the food of Macau? Not to worry—Fat Rice turns the uninitiated into believers nightly. In fact, the restaurant's thriving success led to an expansion that includes a cocktail lounge and bakery next door. Bar seating around the open kitchen gives a bird's-eye view of the mélange of ingredients used in each dish, though servers are happy to walk any guest through the intoxicating mashup of Portuguese-meets-Asian cuisine.

Sharing is recommended for the namesake arroz gordo, a paella-esque blend of meat, shellfish and pickles. Pillowy bread pairs well with crisp chili prawns stuffed with a flavorful blend of fermented black beans and garlic; while chrysanthemum gelée served with jackfruit and peanuts is a sweet and salty thrill.

🔲 2957 W. Diversey Ave. (at Sacramento Ave.)
🚇 Logan Square
📞 (773) 661-9170 — **WEB:** www.eatfatrice.com
🔲 Closed Monday, Tuesday lunch, Sunday dinner   **PRICE: $$**

FLAT & POINT 😊
Barbecue • Rustic

MAP: C3

Rib tips may be the Windy City's cut of choice, but, for now, that's not a priority for Chef Brian Bruns, whose brisket ranks among the best barbecue in town. Rubbed with salt and pepper and then set in a custom-built, 500-gallon barrel smoker for seven hours, the meat arrives so juicy and tender that you won't even want for sauce. Everything is made in house at this ambitious restaurant, from the spicy 'nduja and toasty sesame seed crackers to that smooth pork pâté with maitake mushrooms.

The sleek space, flooded with natural light streaming in from the windows, is decked out with wood beams and logs at every turn. An open kitchen with a hulking grill steals the spotlight in the back; while up above is an impressive list of featured farms and purveyors.

🔲 3524 W. Fullerton Ave. (at Drake Ave.)
🚇 Logan Square
📞 (773) 904-7152 — **WEB:** www.flatandpoint.com
🔲 Closed Monday - Tuesday, Wednesday - Friday lunch

PRICE: $$

GIANT 😊

American • Trendy

MAP: D4

Brought to you by Jason Vincent, this fabulous and friendly restaurant is the epitome of Chicago. Its menu is a listing of familiar dishes (think onion rings, crab salad and baby back ribs), albeit drummed up with unique accents reflecting the chef's distinctive style. The petite space is simple and lovely, with a modern-rustic décor and genuinely cozy neighborhood vibe. A chef's counter in the back offers an up-close-and-personal kitchen experience.

Kick things off with the excellent Jonah crab salad, served with soft waffle-cut potato fritters and freshly made cocktail sauce. Then move on to the "pici with chew, " where thick strands of noodles are cooked to a conservative al dente, and tossed with smoky bacon, chopped jalapeños and breadcrumbs.

🟦 3209 W. Armitage Ave. (bet. Kedzie & Sawyer Aves.)
✆ (773) 252-0997 — **WEB:** www.giantrestaurant.com
🟦 Closed Sunday - Monday, Tuesday - Saturday lunch   **PRICE:** $$

HERITAGE RESTAURANT & CAVIAR BAR 🍴○

Contemporary • Rustic

MAP: D5

As the name suggests, this remarkable operation offers a serious caviar spread at a nicely varied price range, but it's the carefully crafted dishes of Guy Meikle that will have you planning your return visit. The talented chef brings balance and sophistication to Eastern European cooking, intricately weaving Southeast Asian ingredients into staples like kimchi or nam prik.

Dinner might kick off with a wickedly good house-made black bread; or tender, pan-seared pierogis with wild mushrooms, crème fraîche, mustard, and a cherry-black pepper gastrique. Carnivores won't be disappointed by the tender lamb- and shiitake-mandu laced with black garlic, apple purée, and ramp aïoli; or wood-smoked duck paired with hearty Czech dumplings and giblet gravy.

🟦 2700 W. Chicago Ave. (at Washtenaw Ave.)
Ⓜ Western
✆ (773) 661-9577 — **WEB:** www.heritage-chicago.com
🟦 Closed Monday - Friday lunch   **PRICE:** $$$

JAM 😊

American • Neighborhood

                                          MAP: D3

Even in its new digs, Jam remains the sweetheart of brunch-o-philes who won't settle for some greasy spoon. White walls and stone tables punctuated by lime-green placemats give a gallery-like feel to the space; while a friendly welcome and open kitchen keep things homey.

Creative and refined versions of weekend favorites set this kitchen apart. For instance, French toast features brioche slices soaked in vanilla and malt-spiked custard, cooked sous vide and then caramelized in a sizzling pan. Garnished with lime leaf-whipped cream and pineapple compote, this staple is sure to cure any hangover. Eggs benedict, with house-made English muffins bested with eggs, black garlic mayo, spring onion pureé and juicy slabs of pork belly, is a thrill.

- 2853 N. Kedzie Ave. (bet. Diversey Ave. & George St.)
- Logan Square
- (773) 292-6011 — **WEB:** www.jamrestaurant.com
- Closed Wednesday, Thursday - Tuesday dinner   **PRICE: $**

KAI ZAN 😊

Japanese • Cozy

                                          MAP: D5

Despite doubling its space a few years ago, Kai Zan is still the kind of place that needs a reservation well in advance. Located on an otherwise solitary stretch of Humboldt Park, the space is particularly charming and makes you feel like you are stepping into a cozy neighborhood izakaya tucked away in a remote Japanese fishing hamlet. Savvy diners book a seat at the marble sushi counter to watch chefs and twin brothers Melvin and Carlo Vizconde perform their magic up close.

The brothers turn out sophisticated, creative dishes that are decked with myriad sauces, flavors and textures. Non-traditional sushi, nigiri, yakitori, as well as classic bar bites like takoyaki and karaage are all crafted with precise details and impeccable ingredients.

- 2557 W. Chicago Ave. (at Rockwell St.)
- Western
- (773) 278-5776 — **WEB:** www.eatatkaizan.com
- Closed Sunday - Monday, Tuesday - Saturday lunch **PRICE: $$**

LONESOME ROSE 😊

Mexican · Friendly

MAP: D4

Lonesome Rose won't be lonely for long, as it's quite easy to fall in love with her. With big windows draping its space in light all day long, this bright Humboldt Park charmer feels like it was ripped right out of a Southern California postcard—the sun's rays streaming down on bright white brick, blonde wood and a few saturated pops of color.

Brought to life by the folks behind Longman & Eagle, this kitchen's menu features thoughtfully prepared Mexican food, made in-house and impeccably fresh. Don't miss the delicious ceviche, studded with tender cubes of pineapple and pickled jalapeño. Other top contenders have included the tuna tostada, tacos, as well as street corn laced with tomatillo salsa, cotija, edible flowers and a chili "gastrique."

- 2101 N. California Ave. (at North Point St.)
- California (Blue)
- (773) 770-3414 — **WEB:** www.lonesomerose.com
- Open lunch & dinner daily

PRICE: $

LONGMAN & EAGLE 😊

Gastropub · Tavern

MAP: D3

Marked by an ampersand over the door, this operation is the ultimate merging of the Old World and New Order. It's where remnants of a glorious past live in harmony with chefs who prefer bandanas and beards to toques; and the cuisine remains as ambitious as ever despite the room's saloon-like feel.

Although lunch is limited, the kitchen remains busy at all times and the cocktail program—complete with rare Pappy Van Winkle whiskey—is exceptional. Creativity is at the center of each dish, like an addictive pile of Nashville hot crispy pig ears served with a tangy pickle juice remoulade. Dessert highlights like a hibiscus tart features a riff on the key lime pie, and is presented as a sweet mousse with smooth coconut sorbet, topped with crisp coconut chips.

- 2657 N. Kedzie Ave. (at Schubert Ave.)
- Logan Square
- (773) 276-7110 — **WEB:** www.longmanandeagle.com
- Open lunch & dinner daily

PRICE: $$

LULA CAFE 😊
American • Bistro

MAP: D3

This neighborhood darling is just as it's always been. No matter what's on the constantly evolving menu, the fresh, seasonal and original fare keeps it slammed with Logan Square locals from morning to night.

Barbecued wedges of spaghetti squash topped with Asian pear, daikon, and sesame is impossible not to finish. Nicely grilled steaks are accompanied by a tangle of blistered long beans brushed in a house XO sauce with deliciously chewy bits of dried seafood for maximum flavor. Finish with a tall wedge of double-layered carrot cake complete with crème anglaise and a luxurious spoonful of strawberry preserves on the side.

Come on Monday nights for their inspired Farm Dinners and get a taste of what is to come on the regular menu.

- 2537 N. Kedzie Ave. (off Logan Blvd.)
- Logan Square
- (773) 489-9554 — **WEB:** www.lulacafe.com
- Closed Tuesday

PRICE: $$

MI TOCAYA 😊
Mexican • Colorful

MAP: D3

Boasting a lively, charming ambience; friendly, knowledgeable service; and a delicious menu courtesy of Chef/owner Diana Dávila, Mi Tocaya is a welcome addition to the burgeoning Logan Square food scene. Bring friends, order a clever seasonal cocktail, try something from the menu and you'll no doubt leave with a renewed love for Mexican cuisine.

The short but intriguing listing of "small cravings" (antojitos) is influenced by the less-explored Aztec cuisine. Sample dishes like guisado de nopalitos, a fragrant, earthy stew with cactus, zucchini and charred chilies, served with delicious knobs of salt-dusted fried cheese curds and warm corn tortillas. But don't overlook the warm tacos, sure to transport you to the streets of Mexico City.

- 2800 W. Logan Blvd. (at California Ave.)
- California (Blue)
- (872) 315-3947 — **WEB:** www.mitocaya.com
- Closed Monday, Tuesday - Sunday lunch

PRICE: $$

NOON-O-KABAB 🍴

Persian • Elegant

&

MAP: D1

A bustling lunch crowd appreciates the welcoming hospitality at this family-run Persian favorite in the heart of the North Side. Intricate tilework and patterned wall hangings offset the closely spaced linen-topped tables and add touches of elegance to the homey space.

Kashk-e-bademjan is a savory mash of pan-fried eggplant garnished with caramelized onions and yogurt, perfect while perusing the kebabs on the menu. Succulent, hand-formed lamb koobideh and beef tenderloin skewers are juicy and charred with a hint of spice, and vegetarian offerings like tadiq with ghormeh sabzi play up the textural contrast of crispy pan-browned saffron rice against flavorful stewed spinach.

In a hurry? Head across the street to the fast-casual sis for lunch specials.

- 4661 N. Kedzie Ave. (at Leland Ave.)
- Kedzie (Brown)
- (773) 279-9309 — **WEB:** www.noonokabab.com
- Open lunch & dinner daily

PRICE: $

OSTERIA LANGHE 🍴

Italian • Osteria

🛋

MAP: D4

Osteria Langhe offers Logan Square a genuine taste of Italy—Piedmont, to be exact. Partners Aldo Zaninotto and Chef Cameron Grant have created a sophisticated, welcoming and contemporary space, with warm, glowing bulbs that protrude from the walls, bare wood tables and metal chairs lining the floor. Additionally, a communal table at the restaurant's entrance is visible through its garage-like glass façade.

The regionally focused food and wine list celebrates the Italian way of eating ("slow food") with legendary Piemontese pasta like the tajarin, a plate of deliciously eggy noodles twirled around savory ragù, diced carrots and bright green parsley. Dinner specials offer great value, most notably the Trifecta Tuesday $38 prix-fixe.

- 2824 W. Armitage Ave. (bet. California Ave. & Mozart St.)
- California (Blue)
- (773) 661-1582 — **WEB:** www.osterialanghe.com
- Closed lunch daily

PRICE: $$

PARACHUTE ✿
Fusion • Colorful

&

Believe the hype. This eternally packed dining paradise opened to a cascade of critical acclaim, and now nearly half a decade into its life, it's still bringing the goods. What's the secret to this sweet, hip, and low-key Korean-American jewel? For starters, a dinner here feels like you're being welcomed into the home of husband-and-wife chef team, Johnny Clark and Beverly Kim. A young clientele packs the feel-good space nightly, whether seated at tables lining the wooden banquette or perched atop colorful stools that dot the open kitchen-facing double-sided counter.

Though there's a distinctive Korean thread running through the menu, Parachute is an open-ended endeavor at heart. Impeccably sourced ingredients from local purveyors lay the framework, but the team's brilliant application of cutting-edge techniques takes the food to exciting new heights.

You may want to order two of their legendary bing bread, a crispy potato bread fried and baked with scallions, cheddar, and bacon—served with sour cream butter. The feather-light shrimp beignets dipped in aïoli are also a hit; as are those little stacked squares of wood-smoked yuba, topped with peppery arugula and stewed beans.

■ 3500 N. Elston Ave. (at Troy St.)
🚇 Belmont
📞 (773) 654-1460 — **WEB:** www.parachuterestaurant.com
■ Closed Sunday - Monday, Tuesday - Saturday lunch **PRICE: $$$**

QUIOTE 🍴

Mexican · Chic

MAP: D3

Logan Square may be buzzing with Mexican restaurants, but Quiote rises above them for good reason. Warm and inviting, with food that satisfies from sunup to sundown, this restaurant embodies the very essence of a neighborhood favorite.

While the menu's assortment of small and large plates is meant for sharing, the kitchen aims to gratify and will create a typical three-course meal upon request. Expect authentic cooking with a creative twist, as evidenced by dishes such as chorizo verde, a green-tinted pork sausage resting on smashed and griddled potatoes with sweet rings of onion and a golden raisin vinaigrette; or even seasonally inspired plates like the flavorful crab tostada. As for what to drink? Three words: subterranean mezcal bar.

- 2456 N. California Ave. (at Altgeld St.)
- California (Blue)
- (312) 878-8571 — **WEB:** www.quiotechicago.com
- Closed Tuesday, Monday - Friday lunch

PRICE: $$

RAMEN WASABI 🍴

Japanese · Chic

MAP: E4

Who says comfort food must be consumed in humdrum digs? Certainly not Wasabi, where globe lights, sleek booths and towering windows exude modern mid-century sophistication. Down the street from its sister restaurant, which lured patrons for years with the promise of soothing bowls of ramen, this outpost makes it easier to pop in for a quick fix—minus the lines.

Tonkatsu, shoyu, and garlic miso broths bob with springy noodles and ace ingredients, such as pork belly, a six-minute egg, wood ear mushrooms and marinated bamboo shoots. Ramen is a highlight, but it's not the only option. In fact, you may pick from a host of others like pork belly buns, dumplings and rice bowls piled with panko-crusted Berkshire pork, thinly sliced Wagyu or salmon.

- 2101 N. Milwaukee Ave. (at Maplewood Ave.)
- Western (Blue)
- (773) 227-8180 — **WEB:** www.wasabichicago.com
- Closed Monday

PRICE: $

HUMBOLDT PARK & LOGAN SQUARE

SHOKRAN MOROCCAN GRILL 🍴

Moroccan · *Colorful*

BYO $

MAP: C2

Embrace Moroccan hospitality to the fullest and bone up on your Arabic at Shokran, where the country's culinary culture is displayed in a romantic setting. Nooks and crannies throughout the dining rooms offer intimacy; take a seat among the cozy cushioned banquettes and prepare to say "shokran" (thank you) repeatedly as courses come your way.

Traditional dishes offer the most authentic experience, like sweet and savory bastilla, a flaky pastry starter that's large enough to serve two, stuffed with spiced chicken and dusted with cinnamon. Famously rustic, the lamb Marrakesh tagine features a meaty bone-in shank adorned with slivers of bitter preserved lemon and surrounded by sweet peas, whole black olives and tender quartered artichoke hearts.

- 4027 W. Irving Park Rd. (bet. Keystone Ave. & Pulaski Rd.)
- Irving Park (Blue)
- (773) 427-9130 — **WEB:** www.shokranchicago.com
- Closed Monday - Tuesday, Wednesday - Sunday lunch

PRICE: $

SMOQUE BBQ 😊

Barbecue · *Simple*

MAP: C2

Shortly after doors open at 11:00 A. M., the room fills with patrons eager to dig into smoking plates of 'cue. Once inside, peruse the chalkboard menu; then order cafeteria-style before staking your claim among the communal seating.

The half-and-half sandwich, piled with pulled pork and brisket, is the best of both worlds, with chunky shreds of tender pork and spice-rubbed slices of pink-rimmed beef spooned with vinegary barbecue sauce. The usual side dish suspects like zingy, crisp coleslaw and deeply smoky baked beans are anything but standard here, complementing the 'cue as they should. For a sweet finish, look no further than pecan bread pudding drizzled with salted caramel-Bourbon sauce.

- 3800 N. Pulaski Rd. (at Grace St.)
- Irving Park (Blue)
- (773) 545-7427 — **WEB:** www.smoquebbq.com
- Closed Monday

PRICE: $

SOL DE MEXICO
Mexican • Cozy

MAP: B3

Far more authentic than the average chips-and-salsa joint, Sol de Mexico brightens the scene and palate with a lively atmosphere (cue the mariachi music) and delectable house specialties. Walls painted in tropical pinks, blues and oranges are a cheerful canvas for Dia de los Muertos artifacts. To sample the kitchen's skill, start with sopes surtidos "xilonen"—four molded masa cups with a variety of fillings like caramelized plantains doused in sour cream, or tender black beans topped with crumbly house-made chorizo. Then, move on to the pollo en mole manchamanteles, which translates to "tablecloth stainer. " Rich and slightly bitter with a comforting nuttiness, the aptly named mahogany sauce begs to be sopped up with freshly made tortillas.

3018 N. Cicero Ave. (bet. Nelson St. & Wellington Ave.)

(773) 282-4119 — **WEB:** www.soldemexicochicago.com

Closed Tuesday

PRICE: $$

STAROPOLSKA
Polish • Rustic

MAP: C3

Fans of traditional Polish cooking know to proceed to this Logan Square mainstay. If a stroll past nearby Kurowski's Sausage Shop doesn't put you in the mood for some meaty, belly-busting cuisine, then one step inside this old-world sanctum certainly will.

Polish pilsners and lagers are poured at the bar and pair perfectly with the stuffed and slow-cooked plates sent out by this kitchen. Pierogies are a staple and are offered here with a variety of sweet and savory embellishments. Stuffed cabbage is a hearty delight with a meatless mushroom filling, and house specialties may include the light and tender griddled potato pancake that is folded over chunks of pork, bell pepper slices, and braised in a sweet tomato-paprika sauce.

3030 N. Milwaukee Ave. (bet. Lawndale & Ridgeway Aves.)

(773) 342-0779 — **WEB:** www.staropolskarestaurant.com

Open lunch & dinner daily

PRICE: $

TABLE, DONKEY AND STICK 😋

Austrian • Neighborhood

🏵 🍺 ♿ 🍴   **MAP:** D4

When American comfort food just won't suffice, look to Table, Donkey and Stick for a helping of cozy Alpine fare. The rustic inn-inspired setting reflects its reputation as a gathering place where friends meet at the inviting bar or settle in at communal tables for whimsical, creative compositions.

To start things off, peruse the extensive charcuterie selection before tucking into boldly flavored and creatively plated dishes. Layered like a tower, the grilled lamb shoulder over a bed of creamy lentils surprises with every bite. Choucroute garni's rich beefy flavor is cut by the creaminess of the sauerkraut purée. Out-of-the box ideas keep coming through to dessert, where a scoop of pretzel ice cream atop a jalapeño caramel is equal parts spicy and sweet.

■ 2728 W. Armitage Ave. (bet. California Ave. & North Point St.)
🚇 Western (Blue)
✆ (773) 486-8525 — **WEB:** www.tabledonkeystick.com
■ Closed lunch daily   **PRICE: $$**

EATING IN...
LAKEVIEW
& WRIGLEYVILLE

Lakeview is the blanket term for the area north of Lincoln Park, including Roscoe Village and Wrigleyville (named after its iconic ball field). Keeping that in mind, enjoy a boisterous game with maximum conveniences at a Wrigley Field rooftop, like **Murphy's Bleachers**, where hot dogs and hamburgers are chased down with pints of beer. No matter the season, these American summertime classics continue to shape the neighborhood's cuisine. Thanks to a large Eastern European population, sausages and wursts can be found in myriad casual eateries, including **Paulina Market**.

Diners are all the craze in this locality—starting with **Glenn's**, whose menu reads like a seafaring expedition with over 16 varieties of fish. Lakeview has an antidote for practically every craving imaginable, including **Dinkel's Bakery,** which is all about real-deal Bavarian baked goods. Others greet the day with a visit to **Ann Sather**, a sweet brunch spot branded for its baseball glove-sized cinnamon buns.

Stop by south-of-the-border sensation, **5411 Empanadas**. This food truck-turned-storefront sells Argentinian empanadas with such inventive fillings as malbec beef or chorizo with patatas bravas. For a classic American experience, proceed to **The Roost Carolina Kitchen** for a 24-hour buttermilk-brined, hotter-than-hot take on the popular Southern fried hot chicken sandwich.

Cheese lovers make the trek to **Pastoral**, commonly hailed as one of the country's top spots for cheese. Their classic and farmstead varietals, fresh breads and olives, as well as intermittently scheduled

tastings are a local treasure. An offbeat yet quirky vibe is part and parcel of Lakeview's fabric, and testament to this fact can be found at **The Flower Flat**, boasting a comforting breakfast or brunch repast in an actual flower shop. Meanwhile, **Uncommon Ground** is as much a restaurant serving three square meals a day as it is a coffee shop revered for its live music talent and performances Walk just a few more blocks north to find aspiring young chefs with big dreams proudly present a wholesome grab-n-go restaurant called **Real Kitchen**.

Everyone loves a rollicking street fair, and this region's **Shock Top Oyster Fest** featuring an incredible music and beer selection doesn't disappoint. Finally, die-hard dessert fiends should take note: no feast in this neighborhood is complete without a stop at **Scooter's Frozen Custard**. Their creamy frozen offerings are made fresh daily and in a variety of flavors that are bound to delight.

LAKEVIEW
& WRIGLEYVILLE

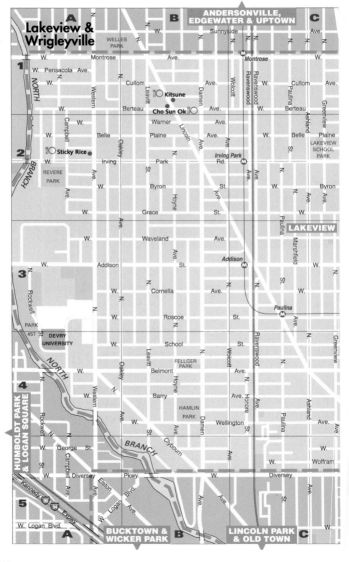

Lakeview & Wrigleyville

ANDERSONVILLE, EDGEWATER & UPTOWN

HUMBOLDT PARK & LOGAN SQUARE

BUCKTOWN & WICKER PARK

LINCOLN PARK & OLD TOWN

Kitsune
Cho Sun Ok
Sticky Rice

WELLES PARK
LAKEVIEW SCHOOL PARK
REVERE PARK
FELLGER PARK
HAMLIN PARK

DEVRY UNIVERSITY
457

LAKEVIEW

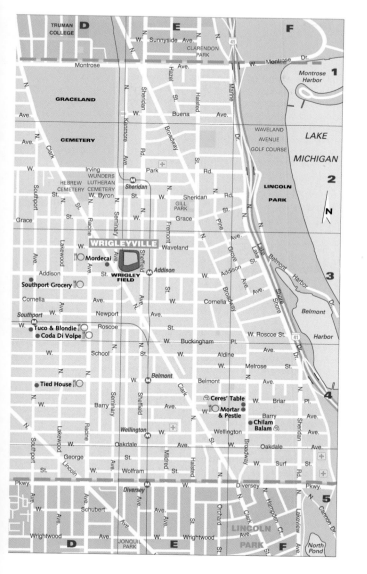

CERES' TABLE 😊

Italian • Elegant

♿ 🛋 🛏   **MAP:** F4

This table continues its reign as a stylish setting for the kitchen's rustic Italian cooking. Whether waking up with brunch, snacking at aperitivo hour or filling up at the bar with the $25 trio, there's an excuse to stop in for any occasion or budget.

Seasonal cuisine featuring simple, elegant dishes made with solid skill is represented throughout the menu. Here, a wood-burning oven turns out a range of top pizzas, as well as mains, such as grilled branzino topped with lightly dressed salad greens and shaved radish. Half-portion pastas are available for the less ravenous, including ridged radiatori tossed with an aromatic oxtail sugo. End with a bit of sweet—as in the Tuscan torta della nonna with baby pine nuts coating a vanilla-custard pie.

🔲 3124 N. Broadway (bet. Barry Ave. & Briar Pl.)

🚇 Belmont (Brown/Red)

✆ (773) 922-4020 — **WEB:** www.cerestable.com

🔲 Closed lunch daily   **PRICE:** $$

CHILAM BALAM 😊

Mexican • Cozy

BYO 🅢   **MAP:** F4

Chilam Balam's cozy subterranean space feels like an undiscovered hideaway, but the secret of this lively Mexican hot spot is out. Though waits can be long, the accommodating staff goes the extra mile to mix up margaritas with BYO tequila or walk guests through the rotating roster of shared plates.

Familiar favorites and seasonal specials make for a festive spread of adventurous, yet universally pleasing dishes. Flat corn tortillas form a sandwich-style enchilada, stuffed with fork-tender beef brisket and topped with crunchy strands of sweet potato slaw. Salty chorizo and green papaya tlacoyos show that opposites attract, and peanut butter empanadas—primed for dipping in Oaxacan chocolate sauce and dulce de leche—take a childhood favorite to new heights.

🔲 3023 N. Broadway (bet. Barry & Wellington Aves.)

🚇 Wellington

✆ (773) 296-6901 — **WEB:** www.chilambalamchicago.com

🔲 Closed Sunday - Monday, Tuesday - Saturday lunch   **PRICE:** $$

CHO SUN OK 🍴

Korean • Simple

BYO

MAP: B1

As tempted as you might be to judge this book by its brisk, unsmiling cover, don't. Instead, enter the cozy, wood-paneled den and raise that first delicious forkful to your mouth.

Take a cue from the regulars and start with galbi, a crave-worthy signature that glistens from a sweet and garlicky soy marinade and warrants good old-fashioned finger-licking. Haemul pajeon stuffed with squid and scallions is a crisp, golden-fried delight; and kimchi jjigae is a rich, bubbling and nourishing broth packed with soft tofu and tender pork. Summer calls for a taste of the bibim naengmyeon—a chilled broth floating with buckwheat noodles, veggies, Asian pear and crimson-red gochujang all tossed together for a delicious reprieve from the city's sweltering heat.

- 4200 N. Lincoln Ave. (at Berteau Ave.)
- Irving Park (Brown)
- (773) 549-5555 — **WEB:** www.chosunokrestaurant.com
- Open lunch & dinner daily

PRICE: $

CODA DI VOLPE 🍴

Italian • Chic

MAP: D3

Though it's named for an obscure wine grape, this dressed-up Southern Italian eatery dishes up crowd-pleasing fare, from wood-fired pizzas to charcuterie and pastas. Its hefty brown leather booths are designed for snuggling into with a group, while the massive front bar draws solo diners to commune with a bowl of outstanding nettle and ricotta ravioli.

Pizza lovers will thrill to the Neapolitan pies, including the classic Margherita as well as a spicy diavola. Served piping-hot from the oven, with scissors for cutting at the table, they're ideal for sharing. But any peace accords may be broken at dessert, when tables fight over bites of the s'mores-inspired caramel budino, with its addictive chocolate graham and toasted marshmallow topping.

- 3335 N. Southport Ave. (at Henderson St)
- Southport (Brown)
- (773) 687-8568 — **WEB:** www.cdvolpe.com
- Closed Monday - Friday lunch

PRICE: $$

MORDECAI
Contemporary • Trendy

🍸 ♿ 🏠 🛋️   **MAP:** D3

Just a baseball's throw away from Wrigley Field, this restaurant is named for legendary Cubs pitcher, Mordecai Brown. Set inside the trendy Hotel Zachary, it appeals to sophisticated diners with its stylish interior, outdoor patio and impressive Bourbon collection.

Crowd-pleasers like fried cheese curds and burgers make an appearance on the menu, but this isn't your usual ballpark bites-kind of joint. In fact, Jonah crab arancini over squid ink aïoli elevate finger food, while roasted trout with yuzu emulsion and crisp, herb-seasoned porchetta have highbrow leanings. Stuffed with caramel popcorn, Bavarian cream, and topped with crushed peanuts as well as puffed sorghum, the crackerjack donut is a delicious riff on the popular stadium snack.

▪ 3632 N. Clark St. (bet. Addison St. & Patterson Ave.)
▪ Addison (Red)
✆ (773) 269-5410 — **WEB:** www.mordecaichicago.com
▪ Closed lunch daily   **PRICE:** $$

MORTAR & PESTLE
International • Neighborhood

🖥️ 🛋️   **MAP:** F4

This charming neighborhood spot is eternally beloved and for good reason. Make your way inside to discover a rustic, farmhouse-esque space that is welcoming and filled with personal touches, like reclaimed wood tables and vintage stained glass windows. As if that weren't enough, the staff is also genuinely friendly—coffee is poured the minute you sit down, and the chefs often appear to greet guests in person.

The kitchen's slogan is "globally inspired cuisine, rooted in tradition" and their globe-trotting ingredients—merguez sausage, cheese curds, romesco—wind their way into a delicious array of brunch-y items. Standards like eggs Benedict and French toast get sweet elevation from unexpected, upscale elements like king crab or even foie gras torchon.

▪ 3108 N. Broadway (at Barry Ave.)
▪ Wellington
✆ (773) 857-2087 — **WEB:** www.mortarandpestlechicago.com
▪ Closed Tuesday, Wednesday - Monday dinner   **PRICE:** $

UNITED

POLARIS_{SM}

business class

Lavish. Luxurious. Polaris lounge. Pick three.

Relax and recharge in our reimagined lounge experience.

fly the friendly skies

SOUTHPORT GROCERY ᵢᵢ◯

American · Simple

MAP: D3

Equal parts specialty grocery and upscale diner, this Southport Corridor hot spot draws quite a crowd. Local products and in-house goodies are stocked in the front of the narrow space, while the rear offers comfortable banquettes for a casual sit-down meal.

Breakfast is served as long as the sun shines, with options like a freshly baked and buttered English muffin stuffed with ginger-sage sausage, a vibrant orange sunny side-up egg and pepper jelly. A side of red bliss potatoes sweetens the deal, but if you're really looking for something sugary, the grilled coffee cake is a double-layered cinnamon and cream cheese delight. Craving more of your meal? You're in luck: certain menu items, denoted with an asterisk, are available for purchase up front.

◼ 3552 N. Southport Ave. (bet. Addison St. & Cornelia Ave.)
▣ Southport
℘ (773) 665-0100 — **WEB:** www.southportgrocery.com
◼ Closed dinner daily

PRICE: $

STICKY RICE ᵢᵢ◯

Thai · Simple

BYO⊐

MAP: A2

Sticky Rice stands out—not only for its focus on Northern Thai specialties, but also for the quality and abundance of dishes made to order. Sunny and citrus-hued, it's the kind of place where those who dare to step outside their satay-and-pad Thai comfort zone will be greatly rewarded.

Luckily, the extensive menu makes it easy to do just that. Tender egg noodles absorb the fragrant coconut curry in a bowl of kow soy that's redolent of citrusy coriander and served with pickled greens and cilantro. Duck larb is zippy and full of spice, with an unforgettable tart-and-sweet dressing. Hint: use the spot's namesake sticky rice to temper the heat while soaking up every last drop.

Food is prepared to order, so speed is not worshipped at this BYOB spot.

◼ 4018 N. Western Ave. (at Cuyler Ave.)
℘ (773) 588-0133 — **WEB:** www.stickyricethai.com
◼ Open lunch & dinner daily

PRICE: $

TIED HOUSE ᵀ◯
Contemporary • Trendy

MAP: D4

Talk about an entrance: a futuristic hallway spills you into this plush "house" whose vast dining room is lined with modern artwork, a marble bar and lounge. In fact, it feels like a deluxe addition to Lakeview, and is the perfect place to enjoy a meal after one of the many events at Lincoln Hall, conveniently located next door.

Chef Debbie Gold helms the contemporary American menu, and diners should start with her "bread service, " which might reveal soft rye, pillowy rolls and delicately sweet oat-porridge bread. Other winners include the "breakfast" ramen studded with lamb bacon, shiitakes and sea beans. A pork pastrami melt is piled to proper Chicago heights, then topped with Gruyère, "secret sauce, " as well as Brussels sprouts- and cabbage-kraut.

- 3157 N. Southport Ave. (at Belmont Ave.)
- Southport
- (773) 697-4632 — **WEB:** www.tiedhousechicago.com
- Closed Monday, Tuesday - Friday lunch   **PRICE:** $$

TUCO & BLONDIE ᵀ◯
American • Colorful

MAP: D3

What's not to love about this cheerful restaurant with solid Tex-Mex fare, killer margaritas—some with mezcal twists—and a soft-serve ice cream machine in the window? The inviting courtyard, complete with a huge fireplace, is the cherry on top.

Grab a seat—outside if you can—and dig into a crowd-pleasing starter like the chili con queso, or the light-but-satisfying crab tostada. Then move on to a mouthwatering taco trio, starring chili-braised short rib, grilled mahi mahi, and zesty chicken tinga; or the steak fajitas, joined by good renditions of clearly not-an-afterthought sides, like beans and rice. While the holy trinity of Tex-Mex cuisine—burritos, fajitas, and tacos—are solid hits, the kitchen can also whip up delicious pork ribs.

- 3358 N. Southport Ave. (at Roscoe St.)
- Southport
- (773) 327-8226 — **WEB:** www.tucoandblondie.com
- Open lunch & dinner daily   **PRICE:** $$

EATING IN...
LINCOLN PARK & OLD TOWN

The congregation of history, commerce, and nature is what makes Lincoln Park and Old Town one of Chicago's most iconic districts. Wallet-happy locals and well-heeled gourmands make reservations to dine at some of the most exclusive restaurants in town, but beyond just glorious white-glove restaurants, there's so much more here.

Lincoln Park's outpost of **Floriole Café & Bakery's** aromas from freshly baked breads, pastries, and cookies never fail to tempt onlookers. For the recreational chef, **Read it & Eat** is a kitchen workshop that doubles as a fully stocked bookstore with a fantastic selection of cookbooks. Check out their calendar of food-centric events—from informative hands-on classes to drool-worthy book launches. Like many foods (Juicy Fruit, Cracker Jack, and Shredded Wheat), it is said that the Chicago-style dog may have originated at the Chicago World's Fair and Columbian Exhibition in 1893. Others credit the Great Depression for its birth. Regardless, the prolific treat can be found all over the city, including at **Chicago's Dog House**, offering both classic and specialty creations. **The Wieners Circle** is beloved for its dogs and fries, late hours (as late as 5:00 A.M.), and intentionally rude service. Carnivores may choose to carry on the party at **Butcher & the Burger**, or linger at **Gepperth's Meat Market**, established in 1906 when the area was mostly comprised of Hungarian and German settlers.

Meanwhile the ocean's bounty can be relished in all its glory at **Half Shell**. Here, the cash-only policy has done nothing to deter crowds from consuming platters of crab legs and briny oysters. Wash down these salty treats with a

cool sip from **Goose Island Brewery**—makers of the city's favorite local beers. Keep up this alcohol-fueled fun with h&rafted punches at **Barrelhouse Flat**, while artisanal goods are on offer at **Blue Door Farm Stand**, an edgy grocery-café. Don't skip dessert when it's deep-fried oreos at **Racine Plumbing**, popcorn from **Berco's**, or chocolate candy and pastries at **Cocoa + Co.**

The Old Town quarter is home to June's annual must-see (and must-shop) Old Town Art Fair; the Wells Street Art Fair; as well as places to rest with beers and a groovy jukebox—including the **Old Town Ale House**. Wells Street is this neighborhood's main drag, and is really where browsing should begin. Any epicurean shopping trip should also include **The Spice House** for its exotic blends, many named after local landmarks; **Old Town Oil** for hostess gifts like infused oils and aged vinegars; or The Fudge Pot for toffee and treats.

LINCOLN PARK & OLD TOWN

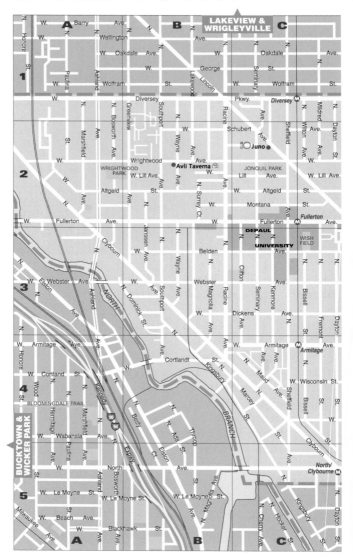

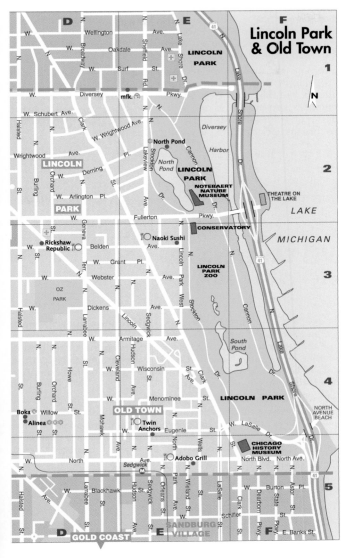

Lincoln Park & Old Town

F

N

1

2

3

4

5

D   **E**   **F**

LAKE

MICHIGAN

LINCOLN PARK

Diversey Harbor

North Pond

NORTH AVENUE BEACH

THEATRE ON THE LAKE

NOTEBAERT NATURE MUSEUM

CONSERVATORY

LINCOLN PARK ZOO

South Pond

CHICAGO HISTORY MUSEUM

LINCOLN PARK

LINCOLN PARK

OZ PARK

OLD TOWN

GOLD COAST

SANDBURG VILLAGE

North Pond

Naoki Sushi

Rickshaw Republic

Boka

Alinea

Twin Anchors

Adobo Grill

Wellington Ave.
Oakdale Ave.
Surf
W. Diversey Pkwy.
W. Schubert Ave.
W. Wrightwood Ave.
Wrightwood Ave.
Deming
W. Arlington Pl.
Fullerton Pkwy.
Belden Ave.
W. Grant Pl.
Webster Ave.
Dickens Ave.
Armitage Ave.
Wisconsin St.
Menominee St.
Willow St.
Eugenie St.
N. LaSalle Dr.
North Blvd.
North Ave.
Blackhawk St.
Schiller St.
E. Banks St.
Burton Pl.

Broadway
Sheffield Ave.
Lake Shore Dr.
Clark
Stockton
Lakeview
Cannon Dr.
Lincoln Park West
Stockton Dr.
Cannon Dr.
Lake Shore Dr.
Halsted St.
Burling St.
Orchard St.
Larrabee
Lincoln
Sedgwick
Cleveland
Hudson
Mohawk
Howe St.
Orchard St.
Burling St.
North Ave.
Sedgwick
Hudson
Orleans St.
Wells St.
Wieland St.
LaSalle
Park
Clark St.
Dearborn
State St.
Astor St.
Clark St.
Geneva Terr.

mfk.

103

ADOBO GRILL 🍴○
Mexican • Neighborhood

🍹 ♿ 🏛 🛋

MAP: E5

Tastefully decorated with lofty windows, red walls hung with evocative Mexican paintings, dark wood floors and a pressed-tin ceiling painted green, this large and lively dining room is much loved. Modern Latino beats (think Elvis Crespo) set the mood for stirring margaritas shaken tableside. Many remember Adobo Grill for its tasty cocktails, but the cooking is just as adept.

Guacamole is mashed to-order before your eyes, with just the right bit of jalapeños to suit your preference. Other dishes show a bit of fusion, like the ceviche de atun made with sashimi-grade tuna, cucumbers, serrano chilies and avocado in ginger-soy sauce. Tacos al pastor offer roasted pork and caramelized pineapple topping fresh corn tortillas. Desserts are pleasantly traditional.

◻ 215 W. North Ave. (bet. Wells & Wieland Sts.)
◻ Sedgwick
℘ (312) 266-7999 — **WEB:** www.adobogrill.com
◻ Closed Monday - Friday lunch   **PRICE: $$**

AVLÍ TAVERNA 😊
Greek • Contemporary Décor

🏛 🛋

MAP: B2

This delicious restaurant has all of Lincoln Park buzzing these days, and for fitting reason. Tucked into a pretty, polished corner space that's decked out with glossy windows up front, this inviting «taverna» also flaunts a curated Greek wine list and nicely crafted cocktails, both of which pair delightfully with its cuisine—complete with a Mediterranean ease and sensibility.

Chef/owner Louie Alexakis wows his diners from the get-go by way of creamy Greek spreads, which are all but mandatory. Crispy kataifi prawns, pooled in Boukovo pepper-mayo, may then be tailed by the moussaka tselementes, combining succulent lamb, creamy béchamel, potatoes, and eggplant. For dinner, go big with the Greek Feast barbecue lamb that must be ordered 72 hours in advance.

◻ 1335 W. Wrightwood Ave. (at Wayne Ave.)
◻ Fullerton (Purple, Red, Brown)
℘ (773) 857-5577 — **WEB:** www.avli.us
◻ Closed Monday - Friday lunch   **PRICE: $$**

ALINEA ✿✿✿

Contemporary • Design

🍸 ♿ 🍴 🈳

Chef Grant Achatz continues to burst with novel ideas at this temple to culinary ingenuity. The kitchen is mature, substantive, soulful, and operates with an infectious confidence.

Whether you are seated at the kitchen table, gallery or salon, dining here is part theater and pure pleasure. Meals take advantage of every sense, so expect scented vapors, tricks, and tableside preparations. The olfactory experience is vivid—if you keep your eyes closed, intense wafts of citrus or smoke will easily reveal what course was just served.

This chamber is packed, and yet, it feels more like a party than a crowd. Service is remarkably knowledgeable and engaged, thanks to a staff that brings both humor and personality to the meal. Dishes are always whimsical and sometimes experimental. Beef rossini, for instance, highlights roasted A5 Miyazaki tenderloin that's presented sizzling-hot, then sliced, and arranged with foie gras. Morels with goat butter emulsion show the beauty in classic simplicity; while desserts like a fanciful caramel popcorn bonbon, bubblegum-flavored Japanese cheesecake, and a green apple helium-filled balloon beautifully illustrate this chef's sense of "nostalgia."

▪ 1723 N. Halsted St. (bet. North Ave. & Willow St.)

🚇 North/Clybourn

✆ (312) 867-0110 — **WEB:** www.alinearestaurant.com

▪ Closed Monday - Tuesday, Wednesday - Sunday lunch

PRICE: $$$$

BOKA
Contemporary · Elegant

MAP: D4

This is the kind of retreat where one can sink in and never leave. The three dining rooms each exude elegance with a bit of romance and quirk—largely thanks to walls covered with ornate escutcheons and whimsical paintings. Against these dark pebbled backgrounds, find plush oversized booths, banquettes, and mirrored light bulbs casting funky shadows throughout the room. The semi-outdoor solarium also has a living wall of moss and ferns. Servers are friendly, genuine, and without a hint of pretense.

Over in the kitchen, Chef Lee Wolen turns out a widely appealing modern menu with a Mediterranean edge. Meals are designed for guests to choose one hot and one cold appetizer, like delicate ricotta dumplings over a verdant purée with thin slices of goat Gouda and fried garlic. This might then be followed by simple-but-elegant marinated cucumbers set over a bed of toasted sunflower seeds and sesame purée. Main courses have included a tender short rib with beef tongue delivering multidimensional flavors.

In the same vein, desserts here make for an exceptionally pleasant experience. Hazelnut and chocolate mousse with a quenelle of caramelized condensed milk ice cream is a classical treat.

◾ 1729 N. Halsted St. (bet. North Ave. & Willow St.)

▣ North/Clybourn

✆ (312) 337-6070 — **WEB:** www.bokachicago.com

◾ Closed lunch daily

PRICE: $$$

JUNO 🍴

Japanese • Contemporary Décor

MAP: C2

Sequestered inside a rather plain and dimly lit space, a bar up front gives way to this more contemporary, bright and airy dining room. The latter is a huge hit among both locals and tourists looking to get all dressed-up for a night out on the town. Its menu offers cool bites like the Juno queen, a special nigiri of salmon topped with scallop and potato crunch, as well as hot delicacies like the honey-glazed quail.

Chef B. K. Park's repertoire of dishes here might include cleverly spun morsels of gently torched prawn with pineapple salsa, and pickled garlic oil-drizzled New Zealand king salmon. Other mains, like soy-marinated sea eel dabbed with ground sesame seeds or spicy octopus temaki, also make a fine feast and are well worth the extra effort.

▪ 2638 N. Lincoln Ave. (bet. Seminary & Sheffield Aves.)
🚇 Diversey
☎ (773) 935-2000 — **WEB:** www.junosushichicago.com
▪ Closed Monday, Tuesday - Sunday lunch   **PRICE:** $$$

MFK. 👻

Spanish • Cozy

MAP: E1

"First we eat, then we do everything else, " said M. F. K. Fisher, the food writer who serves as both the inspiration and namesake for this local darling. Thanks to large windows, whitewashed brick walls and silver-and-white tilework, the subterranean space manages to evoke a breezy oasis. Organized from small to large plates, the thoughtfully composed, Iberian-inspired menu follows suit.

Daily specials are certainly worth ordering, including the clove-infused tender, shredded oxtail. Other simple, flavorful dishes, like warm boquerónes stuffed with marinated anchovies and Fresno chilies, or croquettes with Montamoré cheese and Sherry aïoli are equally tempting. A crumbly slice of Basque cake and an expertly pulled cortado end the meal on a high note.

▪ 432 W. Diversey Pkwy. (bet. Pine Grove Ave. & Sheridan Rd.)
🚇 Diversey
☎ (773) 857-2540 — **WEB:** www.mfkrestaurant.com
▪ Closed Monday, Tuesday lunch   **PRICE:** $$$

NAOKI SUSHI ▮○

Japanese • Contemporary Décor

MAP: E3

Led by Chef Naoki Nakashima, this location is the latest addition to Rich Melman and Jerry Orzoff's LEYE empire. Tucked into a sexy, speakeasy-type space within the lobby of Stratford on the Park, seating here is limited to a handful of tables and a small counter that accommodates six diners.

Snag those reservations in advance because the menu is incredibly delicious and approachable—offering traditional nigiri and sushi alongside carefully constructed maki, temaki (hand rolls), as well as a host of inventive Japanese small plates. Think tender hamachi paired with aji panca, ponzu, and a chiffonade of scallion; or decadent yet ethereally light truffle chawanmushi, finished with a layer of ponzu and a flutter of feather-light truffle shavings.

▮ 2300 N. Lincoln Park W. (bet. Belden Ave. & Fullerton Pkwy.)

✆ (773) 868-0002 — **WEB:** www.naoki-sushi.com

▮ Closed Monday, Tuesday - Sunday lunch   **PRICE: $$$$**

RICKSHAW REPUBLIC ▮○

Indonesian • Colorful

♿ **BYO**   **MAP:** D3

The captivating flavors of Southeast Asian street food are matched by the creative design at this friendly, family-run Lincoln Avenue space. Color and pattern collide as parasols, puppets and bird cages vie for attention with abstract Indonesian wood carvings. Once the food arrives, though, the spotlight shifts to the aromatic plates.

Start with crisp martabak crêpes that hold a savory combination of beef, onions and egg. Then move on to lemongrass-braised chicken thighs in a turmeric-tinged coconut curry with sweet and spicy tamarind sambal and pickled cabbage. Surprise your palate with es cendol, a mix of coconut milk and green pandan jelly in palm sugar syrup. Finally, take home one of Mama Setiawan's homemade sambals to bring color to your cooking.

▮ 2312 N. Lincoln Ave. (bet. Belden Ave. & Childrens Plz.)

🚇 Fullerton

✆ (773) 697-4750 — **WEB:** www.rickshawrepublic.com

▮ Closed Monday, Tuesday - Sunday lunch   **PRICE: $**

NORTH POND ✿
Contemporary • Vintage

MAP: E2

This charming Arts and Crafts building may have started as a warming shelter for park ice skaters back in 1912, but today it is a celebratory and cozy setting that makes you want to light a fire and pop open some champagne. Exposed brick, that roaring fireplace and large windows overlooking the park and namesake pond make the rooms feel warm and pleasant.

A commitment to agriculture is clear in everything: seed packets arrive with the check and each bottle of wine has a one-dollar surcharge that is donated to charities like the Lincoln Park Conservancy or Chicago Rarities Orchard Project.

Chef Bruce Sherman's particular style seems to fly in the face of those minimalist competitors who use menus to list single ingredients. Here, dishes are described comprehensively as a flurry of components that may not always seem to fit together with great success. Try neatly trimmed Arctic char that is slow-roasted for silken texture, then served with embellishments like house-made sauerkraut, mustard seeds, candied walnuts and dauphine potatoes. A duo of strip steak and spoon-tender Porter-braised short rib arrives with pan-crisped black pepper spaetzle, Brussels sprouts and beet-apple purée.

2610 N. Cannon Dr.

☏ (773) 477-5845 — **WEB:** www.northpondrestaurant.com

Closed Monday - Tuesday, Wednesday - Saturday lunch

PRICE: $$$

TWIN ANCHORS 🍴

Barbecue • Vintage

MAP: E4

Within the brick walls that have housed Twin Anchors since 1932, generations have made their way across the checkerboard linoleum floor to throw a quarter in the jukebox and get saucy with a slab of their legendary ribs in one of the curved booths. Though the bar is wall-to-wall on weekends, most weekdays are low-key, with families and groups ready for a casual night out.

Fall-off-the-bone baby back ribs are the real deal, made with a sweet and spicy rub, served with their own "zesty" sauce or the newer Prohibition version, with brown sugar and a wallop of ghost-pepper heat. Classic sides like onion rings, baked beans or hearty chili round out the meal.

If there's a wait at this no-reservations spot, try the beer of the month while cooling your heels.

▢ 1655 N. Sedgwick St. (at Eugenie St.)
🚇 Sedgwick
📞 (312) 266-1616 — **WEB:** www.twinanchorsribs.com
▢ Closed Monday - Friday lunch

PRICE: $$

Look for our symbol 🍇
spotlighting restaurants
with a notable wine list.

EATING IN...
LOOP
& STREETERVILLE

Start your culinary pilgrimage in the Loop, named for the El tracks that make a "loop" around the area, by exploring Block 37, one of the city's original 58 blocks. It took decades of hard work and several political dynasties, but the block now houses a five-story atrium with shopping, access to public transport, and restaurants catering to corporate crowds on the run.

For a quick grab-and-go lunch, **Hannah's Bretzel** is ace. **The Walnut Room**, that Macy's gem, warms the soul with comfort foods, like Mrs. Hering's Chicken Pot Pie—the recipe for which dates back to 1890. Food enthusiasts also flock to **Park Grill**, a full-service restaurant flanked by an ice rink in the winter. Of course, no visit to the Loop is complete without tasting the Italian specialties from **Vivere**, while tourists enjoy eating their way through the city by way of Tastebud Tours' Loop route, whose stops may include **The Berghoff**—one of the oldest known restaurants in town. Equally popular is the Chicago Pizza Tour, also headquartered here.

Bound by the Chicago River, Magnificent Mile, and Lake Michigan, Streeterville is a precious locality that houses hotels and high-rises alongside offices, universities, and museums. Here, Water Tower Place's **foodlife** is a veritable "United Nations of food courts," flaunting 14 different kitchens with everything from hickory chicken sandwiches and deep-dish pizzas to chicken and biscuits. Another notable tenant here is **Wow Bao**, doling out some of the best steamed veggie- and meat-filled buns in town. Hopping skyscrapers,

the famous John Hancock Center is known to many as a "food lover's paradise," but for those whose tastes run more toward champagne and cocktails than cheeseburgers and crinkle-cut fries, there's always the **Signature Room**, located on the 95th floor.

The world convenes at Chicago's lakefront Navy Pier for a day of exploration and eats. **Garrett Popcorn Shops** promises to have you hooked on such sweet-and-salty flavors as CheeseCorn and CaramelCrisp, just as meat lovers know never to miss a beat at **M Burger**. For a bit more intimacy and lot more fantasy, **Sayat Nova** is supreme. Highlighting a menu of kibbeh and other Middle Eastern signatures, this culinary destination keeps its options limited but fan-base infinite. Finally, residents around this way know that Chicago is big on breakfast—and Michigan Avenue's **West Egg**'s breakfast specials (choose between pancakes, waffles, or other "eggcellent" dishes) keep this joint jumping at all times.

LOOP &
STREETERVILLE

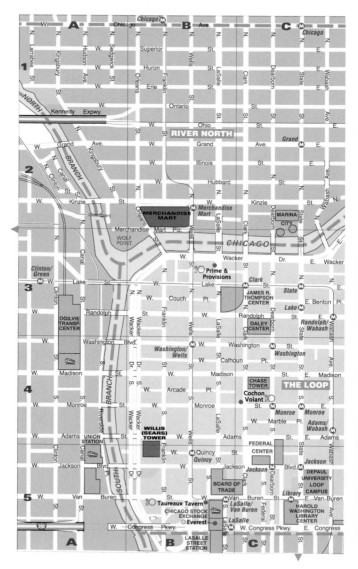

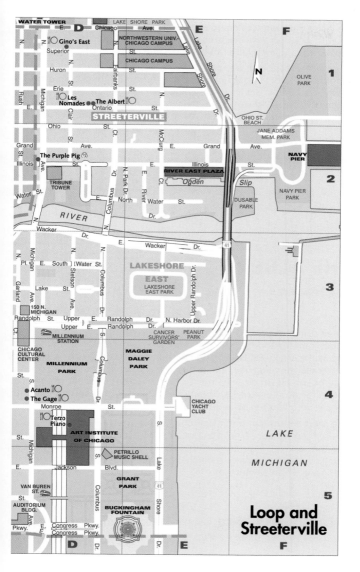

ACANTO 🍴

Italian · Osteria

MAP: D4

This Italian knows how to make an impression: its prime location across from Millennium Park would be a looker any day, but it goes the extra mile with style and sociability. The dining room is dressed up with angular light fixtures and orange banquettes; a luminous marble bar and matching tables lend a masculine, sophisticated vibe.

The carte's standards are as satisfying as they are spot on. Salt cod crochettes sport a golden crust and creamy filling bolstered by mashed potatoes, but it's the fetching speckled earthenware dish that catches the eye. House-made rigatoni tossed with lamb ragù is well-seasoned, complex and perfect for a cold winter's night. For dessert, a fresh ricotta tart is highlighted by bittersweet orange marmalade.

18 S. Michigan Ave. (bet. Madison & Monroe Sts.)
Monroe
📞 (312) 578-0763 — **WEB:** www.acantochicago.com
Open lunch & dinner daily

PRICE: $$

THE ALBERT 🍴

Contemporary · Chic

MAP: D1

Housed in the EMC2 Hotel, this chef-driven dining room has an eclectic menu and mid-century vibe that is perfectly attuned to its namesake, the great Dr. Einstein. The sky-high copper bar is stacked with glass specimen jars and attended by mad-scientist mixologists, assembling clever sips like the Call Your Mother (mezcal, green chili vodka, and celery root). Meanwhile, the décor resembles a chic library, with leather-bound tomes and vintage filing cabinets.

The food churned out of this kitchen is executed with originality and scientific precision, from scallop ceviche accented with yuzu, chili, and topped with a tempura chip, to a plump rabbit sausage with rye berry risotto. Quirky sweets include a cucumber parfait with peanut meringue and strawberries.

228 E. Ontario St. (bet. Fairbanks Ct. & Saint Claire St.)
Grand (Red)
📞 (312) 471-3883 — **WEB:** www.thealbertchicago.com
Open lunch & dinner daily

PRICE: $$$

COCHON VOLANT

French • Brasserie

MAP: C4

Though it's attached to the Hyatt, Cochon Volant is a favorite with Loop locals and sightseers alike for its timeless warmth. Round bistro tables and bentwood chairs are clustered across the mosaic-tiled floor, while a broad, marble-topped bar is bustling with patrons from lunch to happy hour.

Brasserie favorites dominate the menu, ranging from rustic French onion soup to lavish raw seafood plateaux. Steak frites is juicy and flavorsome with a tender prime cut of bavette, offered with five sauce options like a classic béarnaise or rich Roquefort. Breakfast is delicious, but for those who don't have time to sit and stay a while, the takeaway bakery lets commuters snag a pastry (cinnamon or coffee donut holes are never a bad idea) and coffee to go.

■ 100 W. Monroe St. (at Clark St.)

🚇 Monroe

☎ (312) 754-6560 — **WEB:** www.cochonvolantchicago.com

■ Open lunch & dinner daily

PRICE: $$

THE GAGE

Gastropub • Brasserie

MAP: D4

For more than a decade, this expansive, eclectic gastropub has catered to the Millennium Park crowds. Handsome banquettes and columns wrapped in celadon tiles lend a clubby allure, but the space's buzzy vibe never feels overwhelming. While a bar stretching half the length of the restaurant gets its fair share of happy-hour crowds, the rear dining rooms offer a more relaxed setting.

Pub classics with flair define the menu, like malt-battered cod with creamy tartar sauce and parsley-flecked thick-cut fries—a solid rendition of fish and chips. Keep it light with crunchy watercress and sugar snap pea salad with house-made burrata, or go all out with a plate of chocolate-toffee cream puffs garnished with tender cocoa-dusted marshmallows.

■ 24 S. Michigan Ave. (bet. Madison & Monroe Sts.)

🚇 Madison

☎ (312) 372-4243 — **WEB:** www.thegagechicago.com

■ Open lunch & dinner daily

PRICE: $$

EVEREST

French • Elegant

MAP: B5

Summit the historic Chicago Stock Exchange building via a private elevator to reach the sophisticated—though never outdated—scene at Everest on the 40th floor. The sunken-level dining room stays dimly lit by contemporary circular metal light fixtures, all the better to gaze admiringly at the views from the windows framing this formal space. Heavy white linens and abstract bronze sculptures adorn each table, at which smartly dressed guests take it all in.

Alsatian Chef Jean Joho keeps to French tradition on his degustation and prix-fixe menus, with nods to local ingredients among the classical techniques and pairings presented nightly. Where other chefs may feel the need to update and tweak time-honored dishes, Everest celebrates the classics. Subtle hints of ginger in a rich Gewürztraminer butter sauce complement succulent chunks of fresh and meaty Maine lobster. This may be tailed by two thick, bone-in lamb chops featuring ribbons of fat that are toothsome but never too chewy—their richness amplified by a silken spring garlic flan and bed of crisp green beans that soak up the thyme jus.

Cap it all off with tart and sweet pistachio vanilla succès dabbed with red rhubarb jam.

---

440 S. LaSalle St. (bet. Congress Pkwy. & Van Buren St.)

LaSalle/Van Buren

(312) 663-8920 — **WEB:** www.everestrestaurant.com

Closed Sunday - Monday, Tuesday - Saturday lunch

PRICE: $$$$

GINO'S EAST ¶O

Pizza · Family

MAP: D1

Pizza pilgrims continue to make the trek to the original location of this renowned deep-dish chain, where a 45-minute wait is worth every second for freshly baked, steaming pies. The walls, scribbled with years of graffiti, are nearly as iconic as the high-walled pies themselves, whose crusts get their signature crunch from cornmeal and searing-hot metal pans with two inch-high sides.

Filled with heaps of mozzarella and toppings, like the "Meaty Legend" lineup of spicy pepperoni, Italian sausage, and both Canadian and regular bacon, it's hard for some to eat more than two wedges here. The Chicago Fire layers hot and spicy flat sausage, fire-roasted peppers, and red onions for a kicky pie.

Nonconformists can opt for thin-crust pies, but why?

- 162 E. Superior St. (bet. Michigan Ave. & St. Clair St.)
- Chicago
- (312) 266-3337 — **WEB:** www.ginoseast.com
- Open lunch & dinner daily

PRICE: $$

LES NOMADES ¶O

French · Romantic

MAP: D1

Though the casual dining movement seems unstoppable, this elegant holdout still likes to kick it old school. Here, along with classical French cuisine, guests are also treated to suited waiters and cart brigade service. In fact, this quaint two-story townhouse, set in the heart of Streeterville and decked out with throw pillow-lined banquettes, fresh-flower arrangements and an upstairs tea salon, makes for the perfect backdrop. Just past the entrance, find a small parlor and polished bar, which also doubles as a fine perch for a pre-dinner martini in an etched glass.

Come dinnertime, diners look forward to a prix-fixe menu that allows them to choose between various courses, including an ahi tart, warming mushroom soup and sweet Grand Marnier soufflé.

- 222 E. Ontario St. (bet. Fairbanks Ct. & St. Clair St.)
- Grand
- (312) 649-9010 — **WEB:** www.lesnomades.net
- Closed Sunday - Monday, Tuesday - Saturday lunch

PRICE: $$$$

PRIME & PROVISIONS 🍴

Steakhouse • Contemporary Décor

              MAP: B3

Though it would also feel at home in Las Vegas, this glitzy oversized steakhouse fits right in with its swanky Chicago riverfront neighbors. The polished, masculine interior makes its priorities clear from the get-go, showcasing a two-story wine tower and a peek into the dry-aging room under bold, barrel-vaulted ceilings and chandeliers.

A starter of chewy rosemary-sea salt monkey bread whets the palate, while rosy pink slices of slow-roasted bone-in prime rib, rubbed with a crust of fragrant herbs, take a classic hoagie to new heights. When paired with house-cut fries and creamy horseradish dip, it's a meal to rival a Porterhouse. But save room for dessert: a single-serving banana cream pie with loads of whipped cream is a whimsical final bow.

- 222 N. LaSalle St. (at Wacker Dr.)
- Clark/Lake
- (312) 726-7777 — **WEB:** www.primeandprovisions.com
- Closed Saturday lunch   **PRICE: $$$**

THE PURPLE PIG 🐷

Mediterranean Cuisine • Wine Bar

              MAP: D2

No matter the time of day, this is a fave among groups craving first-rate Mediterranean cooking with drinks and a setting to match. Everything is tasty, fun and great for sharing, so go with a posse and get a communal table all to yourselves. The bar is just as nice for solo dining, thanks to the chatty staff.

The menu covers a range of specialties from this region, including panini to a la plancha; and the kitchen turns out flavor-forward dishes that turn simple into spectacular. Need proof? Try the grilled broccoli dressed with an anchovy vinaigrette, roasted garlic and crunchy breadcrumbs. Smoked pork tongue has a noticeable smokiness with just a tinge of sweetness and is served alongside a crunchy Olivier salad with a macaroni twist.

- 444 N. Michigan Ave. (at Illinois St.)
- Grand
- (312) 464-1744 — **WEB:** www.thepurplepigchicago.com
- Open lunch & dinner daily   **PRICE: $$**

TAUREAUX TAVERN 🍴

French • Chic

MAP: B5

This gilded French palace boasts some serious Great Gatsby vibes—down to the classic coupes filled with sparkling Grüner Veltliner and the glowing green lights above the restrooms. Self-made millionaires may splurge on a bone-in côte de boeuf, while the merely well-off content themselves with the exquisite beef tartare, served in a silver bowl atop crushed ice.

The menu tilts heavily towards steak, but its pleasures are consistent across the board. Textbook-perfect roast chicken arrives in a piping-hot cast-iron dish, accompanied by crisped potatoes and a tiny pitcher of chicken jus. An orange-inflected hazelnut torte, with a crunchy feuilletine base, is another must-try.

In warmer months, the garden party-esque patio makes for a pretty perch.

- 155 W. Van Buren St. (at Financial Pl.)
- LaSalle
- (312) 624-8778 — **WEB:** www.taureauxtavern.com
- Closed Sunday

PRICE: $$

TERZO PIANO 🍴

Italian • Design

MAP: D4

Whether you're taking in the modern masterpieces at The Art Institute or simply enjoying lunch and cocktails on the sculpture-filled garden terrace, Terzo Piano is a feast for all the senses. The windowed room is mod and minimalist, allowing the artistry of the Mediterranean-influenced menu to shine brightly at each table.

With Tony Mantuano overseeing the kitchen, Italian influences find their way into many seasonal dishes. Charred tomato crème fraîche lends luxurious smokiness and a tart streak to tender chicken Milanese resting on roasted cipollini purée. And agnolotti bursting with a sweet pea-ricotta filling find savory balance with shards of crispy pancetta.

As an added bonus, museum members receive a 10 percent discount on their meal.

- 159 E. Monroe St. (at the Art Institute of Chicago)
- Monroe
- (312) 443-8650 — **WEB:** www.terzopianochicago.com
- Closed Friday - Wednesday dinner

PRICE: $$

EATING IN...
PILSEN &
UNIVERSITY
VILLAGE

This cluster of neighborhoods packs a perfect punch, both in terms of food and sheer vitality. The Little Italy moniker applies to a stretch of Taylor Street that abuts the University (of Illinois at Chicago) Village neighborhood, and is bigger and more authentically Italian than it first appears. These streets are as stuffed with epicurean shops as an Italian beef is with meat. So, bring an appetite and try this iconic (and messy) Chicago specialty at **Al's No. 1 Italian Beef**.

After combing through the supply at **Conte Di Savoia**, stop for lunch at **Fontano's Subs** or old-school **Bacchanalia**. Parched after a long day on your feet? **Mario's Italian Lemonade** hits the spot, while **Scafuri Bakery** is just the place for sweet treats—they have been baking traditional Italian goodies since 1904. Like any self-respecting college "town," University Village is home to a range of toasty coffee shops. Add to that the mélange of doctors, medical students, nurses, and others working in the neighborhood hospital, and you've got a perpetually bustling vibe. On Sundays, take a break at **Maxwell Street Market**. This sprawling bazaar has over 500 vendors and you might just find celebrity chef Rick Bayless perusing its stalls for dried chilies.

Chicagoland's massive Mexican population has built a patchwork of regional specialties, many of which are found in the south side's residential Pilsen and Little Village neighborhoods. Pilsen is also home to the free National Museum of Mexican Art, the only Latino museum accredited by the American Alliance of Museums, as well as countless taquerias and bakeries.

Birrieria Reyes de Ocotlan is an authentic find for deliciously tender goat meat tacos, but if that sounds too "wild," then **Pollo Express'** whole char-grilled chicken is always reliable. Everyone goes all out for Mexican Independence Day in September, while the Little Village Arts Festival packs them in each fall. And for a Mexican-themed evening at home, **La Casa del Pueblo** is an exceptional supermarket that offers all things imaginable, including household, health, and beauty essentials. Carnivores however can continue to gush over **Carnitas Uruapan's** pork carnitas paired with crispy chicharrónes. Since 1950, **Taqueria El Milagro** has been proffering a unique taste with its cafeteria-style restaurant complete with a tamale-centric menu, as well as a store bursting with burritos and tortillas. And over in Bridgeport, **Maria's Packaged Goods & Community Bar** has been a neighborhood institution in one form or another since 1939. Here, antique collectible beer cans line the space, and leftover beer bottle clusters are being constantly re-purposed as chandeliers..

PILSEN & UNIVERSITY VILLAGE

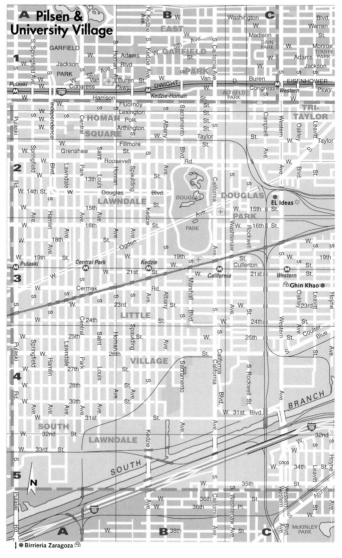

Pilsen & University Village

GARFIELD PARK
Jackson
Adams Blvd.
W. Congress Pkwy.
Van Buren St.
Harrison
EAST GARFIELD PARK
DWIGHT
ALT GELD PARK
SAIN PARK
Washington
Madison
Monroe
Adams
Jackson
Buren
Congress Pkwy.
EISENHOWER
Warren St.
TRI-TAYLOR
Fluornoy
Lexington
Polk
Arthington
Fillmore St.
Grenshaw
Roosevelt Rd.
HOMAN SQUARE
Taylor St.
Taylor
Oakley
Leavitt
Campbell
Western
W. 14th St.
13th
LAWNDALE
Douglas Blvd.
15th
16th
18th St.
19th St.
DOUGLAS PARK
Washtenaw
Rockwell
15th
16th St.
EL Ideas
Pulaski
Central Park
Kedzie
21st St.
Cermak Rd.
23rd
California
Culterton
19th
21st
Western
Ghin Khao
23rd
Oakley
Leavitt
Hoyne
24th
25th
LITTLE VILLAGE
26th
27th
28th
30th
31st
Sacramento
California Blvd.
Rockwell St.
W. 31st Blvd.
24th
25th
Coulter
Blue
BRANCH
SOUTH LAWNDALE
32nd St.
33rd St.
SOUTH
Kedzie
32nd
34th
Hoyne
Leavitt
35th
36th
38th
California Ave.
Washtenaw Ave.
Archer
McKINLEY PARK

N

● Birrieria Zaragoza

124

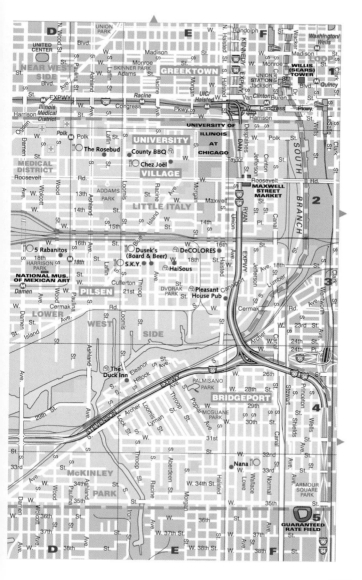

BIRRIERIA ZARAGOZA 😬

Mexican • *Simple*

MAP: N/A

This Mexican institution specializes in a single item—birria—tender stewed goat accompanied by diced onions, cilantro, and house-made salsa. In fact, goat is all that's on the menu, though you'll get a few options as to how to enjoy it: on a plate or in a bowl, in a small or large portion, bone-in or bone-out. Opt for bone-in if possible, as it packs far more flavor.

The bowl option drowns the goat in a generous dose of hearty goat consommé, while the plate is accompanied by handmade corn tortillas for build-your-own tacos, with a small side of consommé for dipping. You can't go wrong either way, but if you're feeling extra decadent, go for the goat quesadilla, a perfect trinity of pillowy tortillas, gooey cheese, and savory goat meat goodness.

🔲 4852 S. Pulaski Rd. (bet. 48 & 49th Sts.)
🔲 Pulaski
✆ (773) 523-3700 — **WEB:** www.birrieriazaragoza.com
🔲 Open lunch & dinner daily   **PRICE:** $

CHEZ JOËL 🍴

French • *Bistro*

MAP: E2

Chez Joël is a tasteful setting beloved by expats recalling their travel stories. Here, walls gleam thanks to a grand chandelier, framed French posters, and ice-blue accents; windows are dressed with velvet; and the courtyard outdoors beckons on warm days. A cozy bar in the back is ideal for sipping, but then get down to business by partaking in this kitchen's cuisine—classic French mingled with global effects.

Begin with such signatures as cuisses de grenouilles à la Provençale—frogs' legs cooked with garlic, spinach and just the right bit of butter. Then linger over a perfect bowl of Gruyère-capped French onion soup. A riff on the rustic coq au vin renders the bird crisp on the outside, juicy inside. Profiteroles or crème brûlée make a divine finale.

🔲 1119 W. Taylor St. (bet. Aberdeen & May Sts.)
✆ (312) 226-6479 — **WEB:** www.chezjoelbistro.com
🔲 Closed Monday, Tuesday - Sunday lunch   **PRICE:** $$

COUNTY BARBECUE 😊

Barbecue • Rustic

MAP: E2

One of the area's top barbecue spots is back in action after an unfortunate fire that forced them to close for two years. The kitchen is still up to snuff and has resumed without missing a beat. Perfectly cooked rib tips—a Chicago classic—and precise slices of Texas-style brisket highlight deliciously smoky flavor and meltingly tender meat. Sides too are a particular favorite and may reveal slowly simmered collard greens or deeply addictive mac and (beer) cheese. Portions are ample but that's why they have to-go containers on hand for customers.

The room is dark and infused with that enticing aroma of char and smoke. Corrugated metal wraps around the base of the walls, while string lights outdoors invite those passing by to make their way inside.

▪ 1352 W. Taylor St. (bet. Ada & Loomis Sts.)
▪ Polk
☎ (312) 265-0836 — **WEB:** www.dmkcountybarbeque.com
▪ Open lunch & dinner daily   **PRICE: $$**

DECOLORES 😊

Mexican • Contemporary Décor

♿ 🚲 🍴 🛋

MAP: E3

This Mexican restaurant's slate-colored walls feature a beautiful rotation of work from local artists, making the pieces a great conversation starter even before the delicious fare hits your table. The lovely bar is yet another bit of artistry, featuring shelves tucked around a series of metal branches; and a wonderful, colorful flower motif on the back wall. A relaxed atmosphere, warm service staff and well-made cocktails seal the deal.

Many of the recipes have been passed down through the family for generations, and one taste of the silky mole poblano, laced over chicken, will transport you back to the motherland. But it's the creative takes on vegetarian dishes, such as the vegan mole or the flor de Jamaica tacos, that truly stand out.

▪ 1626 S. Halsted St. (bet. 16th & 17th Sts.)
☎ (312) 226-9886 — **WEB:** www.decolor.us
▪ Closed Monday, Tuesday - Wednesday lunch   **PRICE: $$**

THE DUCK INN 😳
Gastropub • Trendy

⚏ ▦ ♿ ⛱ ▤   **MAP:** E4

Head to the Bridgeport warehouses, where this stylish, modern tavern—helmed by Executive Chef Kris Delee—feels like a diamond in the rough. Then make your way past the buzzy bar (pouring heady cocktails) to a semi-open kitchen, which is in full view of the decorous dining room, featuring wood tables and mid-century modern seats.

The cuisine may be coined as "working-class fine dining," but there is nothing lowbrow about this menu, which unveils a focused but diverse selection of small plates and mains. Japanese barbecue sauce and sesame seeds are the crowning touch to duck wings, while foie gras mousse with celery fronds and brioche is a study in fine flavors and textures. Of course, regulars know to save room for the Chicago-style duck fat dog.

▦ 2701 S. Eleanor St. (at Loomis St.)
✆ (312) 724-8811 — **WEB:** www.theduckinnchicago.com
▦ Closed Monday, Tuesday - Saturday lunch   **PRICE:** $$

DUSEK'S (BOARD & BEER) 🍴
Gastropub • Tavern

▦ ♿ ▤   **MAP:** E3

On the one hand, Dusek's is a gastropub serving food that is as down-to earth as one of their roasted pretzels tucked with cheese and hot beer mustard. On the other hand, it's just the place to meet for a bite before heading to nearby Thalia Music Hall. The space seems dark and moody, but everyone is having a rollicking good time. Its front room is like a tavern, while the back is a dining room warmed by wood-burning ovens. Menu favorites include a boudin blanc sandwich with beef-fat fries; and bacon-covered country pâté with toasted crostini. Close out with an American mash-up of the classic Paris-Brest, featuring chocolate and peanut butter.

The craft beer selection is terrific with mostly local varietals, so ask your server for pairing suggestions.

▦ 1227 W. 18th St. (at Allport St.)
🚇 18th
✆ (312) 526-3851 — **WEB:** www.dusekschicago.com
▦ Open lunch & dinner daily   **PRICE:** $$

EL IDEAS ✿
Contemporary · Intimate

MAP: C2

PILSEN & UNIVERSITY VILLAGE

Dining here feels like attending an underground dinner party prepared by a merry band of misfit cooks in Chef Phillip Foss' home (he lives right upstairs). There is one seating, everyone is served at the same time and meals are prepaid so guests can linger or leave at their leisure.

The fact that the restaurant resembles a test kitchen is heightened when guests are told to manage their BYO beverages themselves and cooks deliver dishes to your table. Don't worry—they turn the music down so you can hear each description. Yet this is all part of the show; it's a fun, friendly, totally unique experience.

The cuisine follows suit and works wonders by pushing—if not completely disregarding—the traditional boundaries of cooking. Breaking barriers is par for the course: a croquette filled with Caesar dressing set on strips of romaine is to be eaten by licking the plate. Other outlandish surprises include hibiscus-cured salmon with aquachile sorbet, avocado crema and hibiscus gel with a dense chip. Then there is the brilliantly fun French fries and ice cream course, which is designed to look like a milkshake and made in part with a hot potato-leek soup. Once you've had it, you won't forget it.

◾ 2419 W. 14th St. (at Western Ave.)

🚇 Western

✆ (312) 226-8144 — **WEB:** www.elideas.com

◾ Closed Sunday - Monday, Tuesday - Saturday lunch

PRICE: $$$$

5 RABANITOS 🍴

Mexican • Neighborhood

MAP: D3

Located just a stone's throw from the National Museum of Mexican Art, this fresh south-of-the-border charmer boasts a colorful dining room peppered with bright artwork, thumping cumbia music, and a chill neighborhood vibe that makes you want to linger forever.

The delicious authentic food just brings it all home. Chef Alfonso Sotelo worked for Rick Bayless at both Topolobampo and Xoco, and his accomplished resume comes to life in this kitchen. Warm tortillas crafted from heirloom Oaxacan masa are folded around goat adobo barbacoa, savory carnitas, or tender mole enchiladas. Save room for the chocolate tamal—a piping hot chocolate cake served in a corn husk, drizzled with decadent sauce and cajeta, then finished with a creamy scoop of vanilla ice cream.

▨ 1758 W. 18th St. (at Wood St.)
▨ 18th St.
✆ (312) 285-2710
▨ Closed Monday   PRICE: $

GHIN KHAO 😊

Thai • Simple

MAP: C3

The name is Thai for "eat rice, " and you'll want plenty of it to mop up every last bite of this kitchen's perfectly spicy, salty, sweet and tangy Northern Thai dishes. Operated by chef siblings, Nova and Kami Sasi, this is a fun, lively spot, with graffiti-like signage, hip-hop in the background, and colorful murals bedecking the walls. Every item is perfectly balanced, from the crisp and subtly spiced fishcakes with cucumber-herb salad to the glorious nam khao tod, crispy rice with ground chicken, crunhcy pork skin, and plenty of fresh ginger, cilantro and green onion.

As a bonus, it's also BYOB, so bring along a crew of friends with a couple of six-packs, and you'll be able to conquer most of the small menu—along with a few specials listed on the board.

▨ 2128 W. Cermak Rd. (bet. Hoyne Ave. & Leavitt St.)
▨ Damen
✆ (773) 565-4487 — **WEB:** www.ghinkhaochicago.com
▨ Closed Sunday   PRICE: $

HAISOUS

Vietnamese • Contemporary Décor

MAP: E3

This passion project of Chef Thai Dang and wife, Danielle, offers refined Vietnamese cuisine in a plum setting. The menu, divided into five sections, is filled with wonderful, lesser-known (and possibly unexpected) dishes you won't want to miss. The restaurant offers many seating options: an open kitchen fringed with comfy seats; a bar area for cocktails and perhaps an order of those famous chicken wings; as well as two dining rooms, one with communal seating. Don't leave without sampling the goi vit (duck salad); cánh gà chiên (chicken wings with fish sauce, garlic and chili); or eggplant and octopus, laced with coconut cream and fried shallots.

For street food, specialty coffee and quenching cocktails, visit their next-door coffee shop, Cà Phê Đá.

- 1800 S. Carpenter Ave. (at 18th St.)
- 18th
- (312) 702-1303 — **WEB:** www.haisous.com
- Closed Monday - Friday lunch, Sunday dinner   **PRICE:** $$

Remember, stars ✿
are awarded for cuisine only! Elements
such as service and décor are not a factor.

NANA ||○
American • Family

♿ 🚼 ⬜ ⬜ ⬜   **MAP:** F5

Nana Solis is the matriarch of this family-run Bridgeport favorite, whose visible kitchen and two dining rooms (one less formal) seem to be perpetually humming. A devoted breakfast crowd takes up residence at the coffee "bar" and butcher-block tables each day, often perusing the marvelous modern artwork—hung on the walls and usually for sale.

Locally sourced and organic are the guiding principles behind every ingredient here, which is given a bold Latin American bent. Avocado batons are tossed in panko, then flash-fried for a crispy exterior and creamy center. Another staple among the "Nanadicts" is the eggs Benedict with chorizo, corn pupusas and poblano cream. Sunday nights feature family-style fried chicken dinners fit for groups with larger appetites.

◼ 3267 S. Halsted St. (at 33rd St.)
℘ (312) 929-2486 — **WEB:** www.nanaorganic.com
◼ Closed dinner daily   **PRICE:** $$

PLEASANT HOUSE PUB 😊
Gastropub • Neighborhood

⬜ ♿ 🚼 ⬜   **MAP:** E3

Classic English pies may be the specialty of this house, but don't let that inspire visions of chintz and tea cozies—the interior here is decidedly modern, with marble-topped tables and hand-crafted pottery.

But the crowds come for the pies, and for good reason—they're fabulous. The crust is flaky and buttery, and the inside, hearty and satisfying. Dig into the steak and ale, with its beef stew filling and side of minty peas, gravy and mashed potatoes, and you'll be hunting for every last crumb. The comfort food hits also keep on coming, from rarebit mac and cheese with Trooper Ale cheese sauce, to fish and chips on Fridays. Of course, with much of the seasonal greens from local farms, rest assured that even a simple salad will be a revelation.

◼ 2119 S. Halstead Ave. (at 21st St.)
℘ (773) 523-7437 — **WEB:** www.pleasanthousepub.com
◼ Closed Monday   **PRICE:** $$

THE ROSEBUD 🍴

Italian • Family

♿ 🚪 🍽️

MAP: D2

The Rosebud holds its own among the brass of University Village's Italian thoroughfare. The original location of what is now an extended family of restaurants throughout Chicagoland, it's nothing if not classic with its red neon sign, dark carved wood and cool but accommodating waitstaff.

Italian wedding soup brings comfort with tiny, moist meatballs, escarole and acini di pepe simmered in broth; while sweet sausage chunks, caramelized onions and a garlicky white wine sauce make chicken giambotta a satisfying choice. Loyal patrons crowd around white tablecloths for platters of their favorite chicken parmesan or linguine topped with a mountain of clams. Dessert is not to be missed either: a single slice of carrot cake will gratify the whole table.

▪ 1500 W. Taylor St. (at Laflin St.)
🚇 Polk
☎ (312) 942-1117 — **WEB:** www.rosebudrestaurants.com
▪ Open lunch & dinner daily

PRICE: $$

S.K.Y. 🍴

Contemporary • Chic

♿ 🚪 🛋️ 🍽️

MAP: E3

Chef/owner Stephen Gillanders rocks out all on his own at S. K. Y. The moniker strings together his wife's initials, though with his ambitious Asian-accented cooking, it could easily double as a descriptor. Make your way inside this versatile spot to discover a setting that's textbook industrial-chic.

The menu may be slightly motley, featuring everything from cornbread madeleines to foie gras-bibimbap, so if you're having trouble deciding, opt for the seven-course tasting. Not only is it an incredible value but also affords diners the opportunity to tour the kitchen's greatest hits, like seared Scottish salmon with a cauliflower caponata and spicy white shrimp ceviche. A warm maitake mushroom salad with goat cheese is a staff favorite for good reason.

▪ 1239 W. 18th St. (at Allport St.)
🚇 18th
☎ (312) 846-1077 — **WEB:** www.skyrestaurantchicago.com
▪ Closed Monday - Tuesday, Wednesday - Friday lunch

PRICE: $$

EATING IN...
RIVER NORTH

River North not only edges the Magnificent Mile, but is also located north of the Chicago River, just across the bridge from the Loop. Once packed with factories and warehouses, today it is the ultimate landing place for art galleries, well-known restaurants, swanky shopping, and a hopping nightlife. This area is also home to the original **Portillo's**, a hot dog, burger, and beer favorite. Few buildings can rival Merchandise Mart (so large it once had its own ZIP code), known for its retail stores, drool-worthy kitchen showrooms, and two great food shops. **Carson's** is a barbecue institution and just the kind of place where wise guys like to do business—with a bib on, of course! Seafood superstar **Shaw's Crab House** always has crab, naturally, but the kitchen turns out prime steaks too. Take a break from the cold and warm your soul with hearty food and easy elegance at **Lawry's Prime Rib** in the 1890's McCormick Mansion. Indulge your sweet dreams at **Firecakes Donuts** where coconut cream-filled buns may be chased down by hot chocolate. The Windy City's donut craze then carries on at **Doughnut Vault**, brought to you by restaurateur Brendan Sodikoff, who appears to have the Midas touch with this morning fried dough.

Chicago Lights: Urban Farm showcases organic produce, nutritional education, and workforce training, while **Eataly** is an impressive ode to Italian food, employing a massive workforce. This gourmet emporium may present the same delicacies as its New York City flagship, but the Nutella counter keeps the masses coming. Thanks to its diverse community, River North is also a great

destination for a number of food genres, including the local deep-dish pizza. With a doughy crust cradling abundant cheese, flavorful sauce, and other toppings, some may say this is closer to a casserole or "hot dish" than an Italian-style pizza. **Pizzeria Uno** (or sister **Pizzeria Due**), and **Giordano's** are some of the best-known pie makers in town. If a little indigestion isn't a concern, follow up such eats with yet another local specialty, namely the Italian beef. At **Mr. Beef's**, these "parcels" resemble a messy, yet highly addictive French dip, wrapping thinly sliced beef with hot or sweet peppers on a hoagie. Distinguished by day, River North pumps up the volume at night with cocktail lounges, night clubs, and Irish bars. Some may slip into **Three Dots and a Dash**, a retro, tiki-inspired hot spot with well-regarded mixologists; or stop by during happy hour at **Green Door Tavern**. To appreciate what all the fuss is about, order the "famous corned beef sandwich" or the "legend burger" and you'll get the drift.

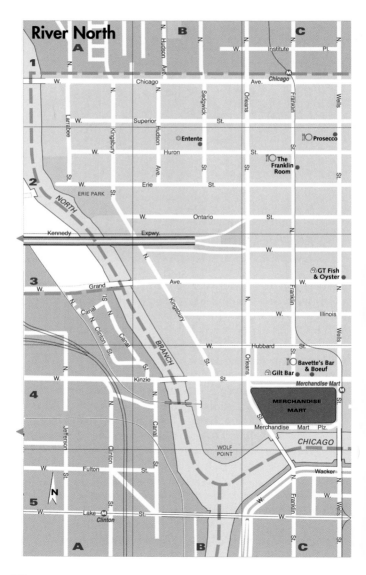

RIVER NORTH

River North

A

B

C

N. Hudson Ave.

W. Institute Pl.

1

N. Larrabee St.

W. Chicago Ave.

Chicago

W. Superior St.

N. Kingsbury St.

N. Hudson Ave.

Sedgwick St.

N. Orleans St.

N. Franklin St.

N. Wells St.

Entente

W. Huron St.

🍴⃝ Prosecco

2

ERIE PARK

W. Erie St.

🍴⃝ The Franklin Room

NORTH

Kennedy Expwy.

W. Ontario St.

W.

3

W. Grand Ave.

Canal St.

N. Clinton St.

Canal St.

BRANCH

Kingsbury

N. Franklin St.

W. Illinois St.

N. Wells St.

🍴⃝ GT Fish & Oyster

W. Hubbard St.

N. Orleans St.

🍴⃝ Bavette's Bar & Boeuf

⃝ Gilt Bar

Merchandise Mart Ⓜ

4

N. Jefferson St.

N. Clinton St.

W. Kinzie St.

Canal St.

N. Franklin St.

MERCHANDISE MART

Merchandise Mart Plz.

CHICAGO

WOLF POINT

W. Wacker

N. Wells St.

5

N

W. Fulton St.

W. Lake St. Ⓜ
Clinton

A

B

C

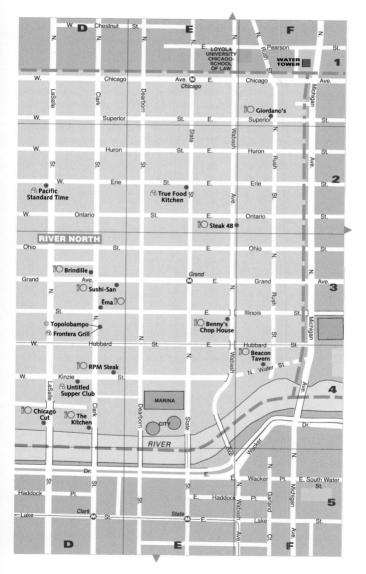

W. D Chestnut St. E N N F N

E. LOYOLA UNIVERSITY CHICAGO- SCHOOL OF LAW

Pearson

Rush St.

St.

WATER TOWER

1

W. Chicago Ave. Chicago E. Chicago Ave.

LaSalle

Clark

Dearborn

Michigan

W. Superior St. E. Giordano's Superior St.

State

Wabash

W. Huron St. Huron St.

St.

St.

Rush

W. Erie St. E. Erie St.

Pacific Standard Time

True Food Kitchen

Ave.

2

W. Ontario St. E. Ontario St.

Steak 48

RIVER NORTH

Ohio St. E. Ohio St.

Brindille

Grand Ave. Grand Grand Ave.

Rush

Sushi-San

Ema

3

St.

Topolobampo

Illinois St. Illinois St.

Michigan

Benny's Chop House

Frontera Grill

W. Hubbard St. E. Hubbard St.

Beacon Tavern

Wabash

N. Water St.

RPM Steak

Ave.

4

W. Kinzie St.

LaSalle

Untitled Supper Club

MARINA

Clark

Dearborn

State

Wacker

Chicago Cut

The Kitchen

CITY

Dr.

RIVER

N.

Dr.

E.

Wacker Pl. E. South Water St.

Haddock Pl.

St.

St.

E. Haddock Pl.

Garland

Michigan

5

Lake Clark St. State E. Lake St.

Wabash

Ave.

Ct.

D E F

BAVETTE'S BAR & BOEUF 🍴⃝
Steakhouse • Brasserie

MAP: C4

With a sultry jazz soundtrack and speakeasy ambience, this swanky destination is unfailingly packed every evening with a boisterous crowd. The feel inside may be dark and loud, but that only adds to the bonhomie of the chic and cavernous den, outfitted with exposed brick walls, mismatched dangling light fixtures and tobacco-brown Chesterfield-style sofas.

Steakhouse and raw bar standards dominate the menu. Most steaks are wet-aged and though some may prefer more funk, the cuts are expertly broiled. Perfectly rendered steak frites served with a buttery béarnaise sauce is a great way to go. But, the kitchen deserves praise for other, more unexpected options like fresh-baked crab cake with remoulade; or creamy short rib stroganoff bobbing with hand-cut pasta.

- 218 W. Kinzie St. (bet. Franklin & Wells Sts.)
- Merchandise Mart
- (312) 624-8154 — **WEB:** www.bavetteschicago.com
- Closed lunch daily   **PRICE: $$$$**

BEACON TAVERN 🍴⃝
American • Contemporary Décor

MAP: F4

Need a place to recharge in between bouts of power shopping? This all-American gastropub, hidden in plain sight right off the Magnificent Mile, is just your spot. Sink in to one of their plush green velvet banquettes for a sip and a snack in this gorgeous space—dominated by an open kitchen with a mesmerizing flurry of activity.

From its dark wood tables to the low lighting, this scene is definitely a luxe one, while the well-executed seafood treats flaunt a rustic sort of refinement. Fortify yourself with excellent small dishes such as shrimp toast or yellowfin tuna tartare. Pan-seared sea bass over a creamy butternut squash purée shows off a familiar flair, and if the banoffee pie is on offer, order it. After all, shopping is a serious calorie burn.

- 405 N. Wabash Ave. (bet. Michigan & Wabash Aves.)
- Grand (Red)
- (312) 955-4226 — **WEB:** www.beacontavern.com
- Open lunch & dinner daily   **PRICE: $$**

BENNY'S CHOP HOUSE ¶○

Steakhouse • Elegant

🍸 🍷 🥂

MAP: E3

Old-school service meets modern elegance at Benny's Chop House. A far cry from the clubby, masculine steakhouses of yesteryear and just a stone's throw from the Magnificent Mile, this expansive but welcoming space goes for understated glamour, with tasteful inlaid wood and burgundy columns offset by natural stone walls, white birch branches, and a marble bar.

Though Benny's steaks are the draw, those prime cuts of filet mignon and ribeye are matched by seafood like a simply roasted bone-in halibut fillet and classic raw bar towers, along with a variety of homey pastas and refreshing salads. A trio of sliders featuring mini portions of Benny's burger, crab cake and sliced filet with horseradish cream elevates the idea of bar snacks to new heights.

■ 444 N. Wabash Ave. (bet. Hubbard & Illinois Sts.)
🚇 Grand (Red)
📞 (312) 626-2444 — **WEB:** www.bennyschophouse.com
■ Open lunch & dinner daily   **PRICE: $$$**

BRINDILLE ¶○

French • Chic

🥂

MAP: D3

This posh bistro is clearly visible to passersby thanks to its large windows and distinctive signage. Hushed and intimate inside, the dining room is awash in a palette of soothing greys and dressed up with herringbone floors along with black-and-white photography. Servers may be casually dressed, but are attentive and engaging.

Brindille's menu bears a strong Parisian accent influenced by the chef's love for French cuisine. Roasted chestnuts are whirled into a creamy soup and poured over compressed apple, wild mushrooms and puffed rice. Spot-on Dover sole meunière is plated with a purée of watercress and golden-crisp pommes rissolées. And for dessert, preserved cherries are just one option to fill the baked-to-order almond clafoutis.

■ 534 N. Clark St. (bet. Grand Ave. & Ohio St.)
🚇 Grand (Red)
📞 (312) 595-1616 — **WEB:** www.brindille-chicago.com
■ Closed Sunday, Monday - Saturday lunch   **PRICE: $$$$**

CHICAGO CUT 🍴

Steakhouse • Elegant

♨ ♿ �"🍴 ⊡ 🖥 🛋 🗒️

MAP: D4

Chicago Cut is a steakhouse perfectly suited for the City of the Big Shoulders. This finely tailored locale bustles day and night, thanks to wraparound windows along the riverfront, sumptuous red leather furnishings, warm wood trim and a crackerjack service team cementing its steakhouse vibe.

Non-meat entrées include cedar-planked salmon with a sriracha-honey glaze, but make no mistake: beef is boss here. Prime steaks, butchered and dry-aged in-house for 35 days, get just the right amount of time under the flame, as is the case with the perfectly cooked-to-order Porterhouse—pre-sliced and plated for each guest. Sides are a must and should include the dome of hashbrowns, creamed spinach redolent of nutmeg or tender stalks of grilled asparagus.

▦ 300 N. LaSalle St. (at Wacker Dr.)
🚇 Merchandise Mart
✆ (312) 329-1800 — **WEB:** www.chicagocutsteakhouse.com
▦ Open lunch & dinner daily   **PRICE: $$$**

ĒMA 🍴

Mediterranean Cuisine • Contemporary Décor

♿ 🛋

MAP: D3

Cross the threshold into this breezy, elegant space—all whitewashed brick, wood-slat windows and lush greenery—and prepare to be transported to the shores of the Adriatic.

The menu boasts an array of fresh, wholesome Greek and Middle Eastern dishes, like a smoky charred eggplant spread, tempting cold mezzes and a variety of kebabs. And it should come as no surprise that these items taste as though they were prepared in a cozy home kitchen, as Ēma translates to "mother" in Hebrew. Dig into the lamb and beef kefta, a plate of perfectly grilled, skewered meat served alongside zhoug, a spicy herb and chile pepper relish. Then cool off with a few spoonfuls of delightfully tart frozen yogurt before booking your return ticket home to the Midwest.

▦ 74 W. Illinois St. (at Clark St.)
🚇 Grand (Red)
✆ (312) 527-5586 — **WEB:** www.emachicago.com
▦ Open lunch & dinner daily   **PRICE: $$**

ENTENTE ✿

Contemporary · Chic

&

From its glass-enclosed corner spot on a quiet stretch of River North to its open floorplan that will have you spying what's on the tables of other guests, Entente may have refreshed its location with new digs, but the signature culinary spirit remains intact.

The kitchen weaves together Indian, Thai, and Vietnamese cuisines in a very convincing and playful way. They never dial down the intensity—one bite of the fluke buried under fresh passionfruit granita and curry powder and you'll soon be hip to their style. Each dish delivers a remarkable mouthful, and most of the kitchen's creations are rich, as well as unexpected. Foie gras served with warm banana bread and cocoa nibs is decadently delicious; seared scallop and roe served with yuzu curd and a palate-cleansing citrus salad is bright and clever; and monkfish set in a Benton's bacon broth hits the mark with balanced flavors.

It's a steady stream of hits all the way to dessert. Thai iced tea, served as a panna cotta with coconut pop rocks, fingerlime sorbet, and meringue, shows off their flair for whimsy, but that mango panna cotta with Thai-basil granita and charred Japanese sushi rice is a complete and utter showstopper.

◼ 700 N. Sedgwick St. (at Huron St.)

▥ Chicago (Franklin)

☏ (312) 285-2247 — **WEB:** www.ententechicago.com

◼ Closed lunch daily

PRICE: $$$

THE FRANKLIN ROOM 🍴

American • Tavern

♿ 🛏 🍽 🕯

MAP: C2

With a motto like "Ladies and Gentlemen Welcome, " it's no surprise that the subterranean space housing this modern-day tavern and whiskey bar is as inviting as they come. Surrounded by backlit bottles of top-notch spirits under wrought-iron latticework light panels, guests gather for convivial conversation and great drinks.

Fans of Bourbon will delight in the Derby Day Mule, which swaps out vodka for Buffalo Trace. Brown spirits are celebrated; note that hefty supply of Pappy Van Winkle. Pair your libation with a snack of parmesan-battered cauliflower tots with blue cheese dressing before tucking in to the delightfully rich squid ink seafood pasta tossed in a pesto cream sauce. End on a high note—think Bourbon-infused milkshake with house-made ice cream.

▨ 675 N. Franklin St. (bet. Erie & Huron Sts.)
🚇 Chicago (Brown)
☎ (312) 445-4686 — **WEB:** www.franklinroom.com
▨ Open lunch & dinner daily   **PRICE: $$**

FRONTERA GRILL 😊

Mexican • Colorful

🍸 🛏 🍽 🛎 🕯

MAP: D3

This linchpin in Rick Bayless' empire is decidedly unique in its homage to regional Mexican cuisine and displays a cult-like devotion to local product. Service at this dining room, psychedelic in its color scheme, can verge on vapid, but find a seat on the bar side for a warmer (and worthier) experience.

The ever-changing menu is cohesive, highlighting everything from the ceviches of Baja to the moles of Oaxaca. Begin with the sopa azteca—a nourishing pasilla chile broth poured atop tortilla strips, avocado, grilled chicken and jack cheese. A version of the classic from Morelia, enchiladas a la plaza are first flash-fried, then folded over seasoned cabbage, potatoes and carrots. Pair this with a side of spinach in green chile and you won't be unhappy.

▨ 445 N. Clark St. (bet. Hubbard & Illinois Sts.)
🚇 Grand (Red)
☎ (312) 661-1434 — **WEB:** www.rickbayless.com
▨ Closed Sunday - Monday   **PRICE: $$**

GILT BAR
Gastropub • Brasserie

MAP: C4

It's not easy to miss the revolving door entrance to Gilt Bar, a moody and imposing retreat. The bar up front mixes cocktails to a metronomic rhythm, while the back feels more intimate with studded leather banquettes and nostalgic lighting.

However, make no mistake, this is no Bugsy Malone speakeasy, but a grown-up version for aficionados with astute palates. Snack on smoky Brussels sprouts finished with a Dijon vinaigrette and dusting of pecorino, before savoring ricotta gnocchi tossed in a nutty brown butter sauce with butternut squash, chives and parmesan. For the finale, diner-style pies are all the rage. Gorge on a coconut-cream rendition topped with pleasantly bitter coffee-infused ice cream and chocolate sauce—perhaps to the tunes of Bob Dylan? Bliss.

230 W. Kinzie St. (at Franklin St.)
Merchandise Mart
(312) 464-9544 — **WEB:** www.giltbarchicago.com
Closed lunch daily

PRICE: $$

GIORDANO'S
Pizza • Family

MAP: F1

Value, friendly service, and iconic deep-dish pizza make Giordano's a crowd sweetheart among residents and tourists alike. With locations dotting the city and suburbs, this spot has been gratifying locals with comforting Chicago-style Italian-American fare for years. Come during the week—service picks up especially at dinner—to avoid the cacophony.

The menu includes your typical salads and pastas, but you'd do well to save room for the real star: the deep-dish. Bring backup because this pie could feed a small country. The spinach version arrives on a buttery pastry crust, filled with sautéed (or steamed) spinach with tomato sauce and topped with mozzarella and parmesan. For those cold, windy nights, opt for delivery—their website sketches a detailed menu.

730 N. Rush St. (at Superior St.)
Chicago (Red)
(312) 951-0747 — **WEB:** www.giordanos.com
Open lunch & dinner daily

PRICE: $

GT FISH & OYSTER 😋
Seafood • Chic

MAP: C3

Quaint seaside shacks have nothing on this nautical-chic spot. A boomerang-shaped communal table by the raw bar makes a perfect perch for slurping oysters. Lead fishing weights keep napkins in place on brass-edged tables, arranged beneath a chalkboard mural of a jaunty swordfish skeleton. Pescatarians savor the fish dishes meant for sharing—start with snapper ceviche tossed with mashed avocado, tarragon, and served with corn tostadas as well as a salad of frisée and shaved radish. Then move on to a sterling, golden-hued mille feuille, starring layers of puff pastry with piped dots of a cream cheese custard, diced pineapple, and lime sorbet off to one side.

Steak lovers should stop by GT Prime, frequented for its luxurious setting and unique cuts of meat.

- 531 N. Wells St. (at Grand Ave.)
- Grand (Red)
- (312) 929-3501 — **WEB:** www.gtoyster.com
- Open lunch & dinner daily

PRICE: $$

THE KITCHEN 🍴
American • Chic

MAP: D4

Panoramic views and eye-popping spaces are par for the course at most of the lofty spots abutting the Chicago River, but The Kitchen's farm-to-table food manages to steer the focus back to the plate. The restaurant's approachable, community-minded take on straightforward seasonal food—along with its impressive drinks program—makes it easy to please.

Even if you're not attending a Monday "Community Night" dinner alongside many of the purveyors whose ingredients appear on the plate, you'll find a fresh, flavorful mix of dishes. Crushed white bean bruschetta is topped with a sprightly herb and frisée salad, which is in turn dressed with a blood orange vinaigrette. And wild Bristol Bay salmon is poached with care, its silkiness punctuated by garlic-chive aïoli.

- 316 N. Clark St. (bet. Kinzie St. & the Chicago River)
- Merchandise Mart
- (312) 836-1300 — **WEB:** www.thekitchenbistros.com
- Open lunch & dinner daily

PRICE: $$

PACIFIC STANDARD TIME 😊

Californian · Trendy

                                           MAP: D2

Reservations are recommended at this buzzy Cal-Italian spot. Awash in bright white walls and blonde wood, including a bustling bar settled into the center of the restaurant, Pacific Standard Time brings a breezy West Coast vibe to River North, and the Midwest can't get enough.

On the menu, you'll find a refreshing mix of Neapolitan-style pizzas, homemade pastas and fish. Highlights though include the ahi tuna starter, as well as trout dressed with a Thai vinaigrette, sesame, avocado purée and dill. At the center of the kitchen are two oak wood-fueled hearths, which turn out rib-sticking items like roasted chicken and whole duck (not to mention those delicious pies).

Service is personable and casual, but highly attentive to the details that count.

- 141 W. Erie St. (at LaSalle Dr.)
- Grand
- (312) 736-1778 — **WEB:** www.pstchicago.com
- Closed Saturday lunch   **PRICE: $$**

PROSECCO 🍴

Italian · Elegant

                                           MAP: C2

No matter the hour, it's always time for bubbly at Prosecco, where a complimentary splash of the namesake Italian sparkler starts each meal. This fizzy wine inspires the restaurant's elegant décor, from creamy pale walls and damask drapes to travertine floors. Sit at the long wooden bar or in one of the well-appointed dining rooms for a second glass chosen from the long list of frizzante and spumante wines.

Hearty dishes spanning the many regions of Italy cut through the heady bubbles. Carpaccio selections include the classic air-dried bresaola as well as whisper-thin seared rare duck breast. Saltimbocca di vitello marries tender veal medallions with crispy Prosciutto di Parma and creamy mozzarella, with hints of sage in the tomato-brandy sauce.

- 710 N. Wells St. (bet. Huron & Superior Sts.)
- Chicago (Brown)
- (312) 951-9500 — **WEB:** www.prosecco.us.com
- Closed lunch daily   **PRICE: $$**

RPM STEAK 🍴

Steakhouse • Trendy

MAP: D4

This bi-level space, centered around a large wraparound marble bar, flaunts a warm, sleek, and moneyed vibe. The polished black- white- and wood-décor speaks to the finer things in life, with a menu of succulent steaks, shellfish, and sides to boot. There's always a full house; for the best people-watching, score one of the semicircular booths. While the aging process and cuts on offer keep spinning, expect to find Japanese prefectures and solid American producers. Highlights include classic steak frites, petite filets, and that mighty cowboy steak—cooked to pink and seasoned with a winning blend of ground and fried thyme, rosemary, garlic, and kosher salt.

The wine list meanders around the globe with nods to Napa, Burgundy, and everything in between.

- 66 W. Kinzie St. (bet. Clark & Dearborn Sts.)
- Merchandise Mart
- (312) 284-4990 — **WEB:** www.rpmsteak.com
- Closed Saturday - Sunday lunch   **PRICE: $$$$**

STEAK 48 🍴

Steakhouse • Trendy

MAP: E2

Steakhouses are as prevalent as the Chicago wind in River North, but the family that founded the much-loved Mastro's shows us that they've still got some tricks up their sleeves with this popular sibling. Don't be fooled by the buzzing crowd and thumping music as Steak 48—albeit trendy—really knows how to pack them in by doling out sizzling, next-level cuts with impressive consistency.

The interior is dark, with black floors, burnt-orange booths and a sparkling glass-enclosed kitchen that showcases a massive display of seafood on ice. Well-priced and appetizing cuts of meat are the main attraction, but their notable supporting lineup of a dozen sides may include delicious double-baked truffle potatoes, generous salads and myriad fish preparations.

- 615 N. Wabash Ave. (bet. Ohio & Ontario Sts.)
- Grand (Red)
- (312) 266-4848 — **WEB:** www.steak48.com
- Closed lunch daily   **PRICE: $$$**

SUSHI-SAN ⅋◐

Japanese • *Minimalist*

&

MAP: D3

Why cook dinner when it's all too easy to drop into this sleek retreat for a quick bite or linger with friends over sake and sips? One of the few spots in town that is open late, Sushi-San's menu is built for crowds—imagine the likes of filling rice bowls and extensive lists of maki. Charcoal-grilled proteins and vegetables, like the delicious Vietnamese Berkshire pork or charred cauliflower, also make for true-blue feasts.

The interior is hip and minimalist, furnished with wooden seats, exposed ductwork, a black ceiling and pumping hip-hop beats. A counter in the back is best for a more intimate experience with the chef. Service is friendly and efficient; and if in a rush, rest easy, as you could be in and out in under half an hour if need be.

■ 63 W. Grand Ave. (bet. Clark & Dearborn Sts.)
🚇 Grand (Red)
℘ (312) 828-0575 — **WEB:** www.sushisanrestaurant.com
■ Closed Sunday lunch

PRICE: $$

TRUE FOOD KITCHEN 👻

American • *Contemporary Décor*

& ⌫

MAP: E2

True Food Kitchen is just what the doctor ordered—Dr. Andrew Weil, that is, who, along with "restopreneur" Sam Fox, has written a prescription for food that is as healthy as it is delicious.

Housed in a trendy part of the city and in an 8,000-square-foot, loft-like space, this open and airy "kitchen" features lime-green banquettes, lemon-hued chairs and a bar that slings fresh juice cocktails like skinny citrus margaritas. The menu showcases the chef's talent for delivering next-level vegetable dishes. But carnivores may rest easy as the gluten-free chicken sausage pie, as well as the spaghetti squash casserole topped with fresh mozzarella and dressed with herbs, caramelized onions and shredded zuchinni, are bound to sate every type of palate.

■ 1 W. Erie St. (at State St.)
🚇 Grand (Red)
℘ (312) 204-6981 — **WEB:** www.truefoodkitchen.com
■ Open lunch & dinner daily

PRICE: $$

TOPOLOBAMPO ✿

Mexican • *Elegant*

MAP: D3

This jewel in Rick Bayless' crown welcomes a rush of serious diners for original south-of-the-border food with an upscale twist. While you have to walk through cacophonous Frontera Grill, the relative serenity that greets you is worth the detour. This bright and cheery dining room with gold curtains and colorful artwork feels worlds away from the fiesta up front.

The regional Mexican cuisine boasts a panoply of flavors, colors and textures with a finesse that is truly impressive. Lunches are laid-back and may include a quartet of quesadillas stuffed with chorizo, black beans and queso fresco. These are made even more luscious when served with a Veracruz salsa negra. Seasonal or classic tasting menus at dinner demonstrate the kitchen's haute cuisine approach to authentic items and ingredients. Dishes are also sauced perfectly: the uni-infused spicy yellow mole poured over a single seared scallop is just one example.

Cocktails are noteworthy (margaritas, naturally), with tequila and mezcal flights, plus a concise wine list featuring Mexican labels. Teetotalers get equal attention thanks to sweet and tangy agua frescas splashed with tropical juices that are among the best in town.

■ 445 N. Clark St. (bet. Hubbard & Illinois Sts.)

▣ Grand (Red)

✆ (312) 661-1434 — **WEB:** www.rickbayless.com

■ Closed Sunday - Monday, Saturday lunch   **PRICE: $$$$**

UNTITLED SUPPER CLUB

Contemporary · Trendy

MAP: D4

An unmarked entrance leads the way to this subterranean lair, its various rooms pumping out music and serving up hand-crafted cocktails to a cool clientele lounging in tufted leather banquettes. Lights are sultry, tables are low-slung and casual, and there are no less than 507 whiskeys to choose from.

A charcuterie board may offer up silky duck rillettes, shot through with foie gras; textured and spreadable liverwurst; as well as thin slices of prosciutto and coppa accompanied by a house-made mostarda. Overstuffed squash blossom rellenos are filled with creamy ricotta and served over agave-spiked corn relish as well as chili-lime crema. Don't miss the scrumptious meatloaf sandwich, slathered with Korean-style ketchup and laced with rosemary-infused aïoli.

■ 111 W. Kinzie St. (bet. Clark & LaSalle Sts.)

▣ Merchandise Mart

✆ (312) 880-1511 — **WEB:** www.untitledchicago.com

■ Closed Sunday, Monday - Saturday lunch   **PRICE:** $$

Look for our symbol 🍸
spotlighting restaurants
with a serious cocktail list.

EATING IN...
WEST LOOP

Once home to scores of warehouses and smoke-spewing factories, the West Loop today is arguably the most booming part of the Windy City, whirring with sleek art galleries, attractive lofts, hopping nightclubs, and cool, cutting-edge restaurants.

Young residents may have replaced the struggling immigrants of yore; nevertheless, traces of ethnic flavor can still be found along these vibrant blocks. They certainly aren't as dominant as before—what a difference a century or two can make—but nearby Taylor Street continues to charm passersby, tourists, and residents alike with its timeless-turned-slightly kitschy feel. Imagine the likes of delis, groceries, and food stops galore and you will start to get the picture. For tasty, Mediterranean-inspired munching, make your way to Greektown, where everybody's Greek, even if it's just for the day.

Shout "opa" at the **Taste of Greektown** festival, held each August, and proffering thrilling eats as well as drinks from local restaurants, and celebrating all things Mediterranean. If all this sounds too Greek to you, then venture beyond into "Restaurant Row," situated along Randolph Street. Here, culinary treasures hide among beautiful, fine dining establishments.

Whet your appetite with everything from sushi to hefty subs. In fact, this mile-long sandwich breed is a best seller bursting with salty meats at **J.P. Graziano's**. Yes, the queues are long and crowds pack this spot, but rest assured that the wait is entirely worth it. If all else fails, round-up say 1,000 of your closest friends for a meze feast at one of the many Moroccan spots nearby. Late night revelers may choose to continue the party at **CH Distillery**, which is known to cull the

finest spirits in-house, just as hoops fans whoop it up during Bulls games at the United Center—also home to the Blackhawks. Depending on the score, the most exciting part of the night is post-game, binging with buddies over beers and a spectrum of bar bites. Speaking of which, everybody knows your name at **The Aberdeen Tap**, a local watering hole renowned for its deliciously varied pub grub (from shrimp tacos to Cajun-smoked gator), outdoor patio when the weather is right, and massive selection (over 65 brews) of beers on tap. But, be sure to take your more finicky pals to **Rhine Hall**, a boutique brandy distillery run by a father-and-daughter duo. Finally, those who prefer a little brawl with their beer are bound to fall for **Twisted Spoke**, the proverbial biker bar with tattoos and 'tudes to match. The music is loud and the drinks are plentiful, but it's all meant in good testosterone- and alcohol-fueled fun.

WEST LOOP

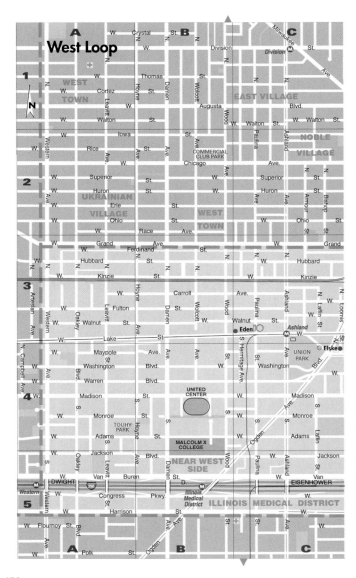

West Loop

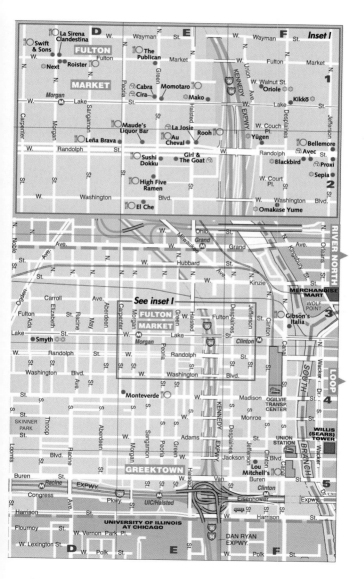

Inset I

D W. Wayman St. E W. Wayman F

La Sirena Clandestina
Swift & Sons
FULTON
Next **Roister**
W. Fulton
The Publican
W. Market
N. Union
W. Walnut St.
Oriole
W. Fulton Market

MARKET

N. Peoria
N. Green
Cabra
Cira
Momotaro
Mako

Morgan
W. Lake St.
N. Halsted
N. Desplaines
N. Jefferson
Lake St.
Kikkō

Carpenter
Morgan
Sangamon

Maude's Liquor Bar
St.
La Josie
W. Couch Pl.
Yügen

Leña Brava
Au Cheval
Rooh
Bellemore
W. Randolph St.
W. Randolph St.
Avec
Proxi

Sushi Dokku
Girl & The Goat
Blackbird
Sepia

W. Court Pl.

High Five Ramen
Blvd.
W. Washington Blvd.
W. Washington

El Che
Omakase Yume

RIVER NORTH

W. Ohio St.
Milwaukee
Grand
Grand
Ave.
Orleans

N. Noble
Ave.
W. Hubbard
Ave.
N. Kingsbury
St.

N. Ogden
Ave.
Carroll
Ave.
Aberdeen
May
Racine
Morgan
Green
Halsted
Fulton
Desplaines
Jefferson
Clinton
Canal
St.
Kinzie

MERCHANDISE MART
WOLF POINT

See inset I

Fulton
Ada
Elizabeth
St.
Racine
FULTON MARKET
Carpenter
Green
Halsted
Fulton
Desplaines
Gibson's Italia

Lake St.
Smyth
Morgan
Lake
Clinton
St.

SOUTH BRANCH
LOOP

W. Randolph St.
Randolph
St.

W. Washington
Washington
Blvd.

Monteverde

WILLIS (SEARS) TOWER

SKINNER PARK
Throop
St.
Aberdeen
Sangamon
Peoria
Green
Madison
OGILVIE TRANSP. CENTER
Monroe

St. Loomis
Blvd.
Racine
Adams
St.
UNION STATION
Jackson
Jefferson
Clinton
Canal
Blvd.

Buren
St.
GREEKTOWN
Van
Lou Mitchell's
Buren

Racine
EXPWY.
Halsted
Clinton
Congress
Pkwy.
UIC/Halsted
Eisenhower
Expwy.

Harrison
St.
Harrison
St.

Flournoy
St.
UNIVERSITY OF ILLINOIS AT CHICAGO
DAN RYAN EXPWY.

W. Lexington St.
W. Vernon Park Pl.

D W. Polk St. E St. F St.

AU CHEVAL

American · Tavern

MAP: E2

This corner bar on Randolph Street's restaurant row may be dim, but it's got a few glittering edges. The reel-to-reel in the doorway lends a retro feel, but the rest is decidedly cushy. Good thing too, since patrons often wait up to two hours just to snag a seat here. Bartenders work just as hard as line cooks until the wee hours.

Burgers are all the (overhyped) rage here, but leave them to the masses and order chilaquiles or the 32-ounce pork Porterhouse. This kitchen puts a highfalutin spin on simple dishes: think foie gras folded into scrambled eggs and house-made sausages for bologna sandwiches that go beyond a kid's wildest dreams. The crispy fries with Mornay sauce and garlic aïoli topped with a fried egg are a good bet no matter the time of day.

- 800 W. Randolph St. (at Halsted St.)
- Morgan
- (312) 929-4580 — **WEB:** www.auchevalchicago.com
- Open lunch & dinner daily

PRICE: $$

AVEC 😊

Mediterranean Cuisine · Contemporary Décor

MAP: F2

Fans have been clamoring for the dinner plates at this West Randolph mainstay for more than a decade—and now that lunch is on the menu, it's official: Avec is a non-stop hangout. It's a fun vibe, as diners are tightly packed at a long counter with communal seats in the chic wood plank-encased room; servers do a good job attending to the crowd.

Mediterranean flavors factor prominently in the kitchen's stimulating creations, like a kale and carrot salad dressed with delightfully herbaceous and spicy green harissa as well as sunflower seeds for crunch. A thick slice of excellent whole grain bread spread with walnut-beet muhamarra is the foundation of an open-faced roasted salmon sandwich. Other delights—there are many—come and go with the seasons.

- 615 W. Randolph St. (bet. Desplaines & Jefferson Sts.)
- Clinton (Green/Pink)
- (312) 377-2002 — **WEB:** www.avecrestaurant.com
- Closed Saturday lunch

PRICE: $$

BELLEMORE 🍴

Contemporary • Luxury

🍸 🍹 ♿

MAP: F2

The good folks at the Boka Restaurant Group have done it again with Bellemore, a West Loop beauty that has tongues wagging across town. Headed by the extremely talented Jimmy Papadopoulos (of Bohemian House), this menu pairs the most pristine ingredients with classical French techniques. Unsurprisingly, the results practically shine in dishes like venison tartare, paired with silky bonito aïoli, smoky trumpet mushrooms and Tokyo turnips; or a perfectly flaky oyster pie, starring caviar, crème fraîche and tart green apple.

The servers are jacketed, yet their style is friendly and personable. The buzzy interior lights up at night with convivial chatter, as guests soak in the stunning setting, lined with rounded booths and striking chandeliers.

▪ 564 W. Randolph St. (at Jefferson St.)
🚇 Clinton (Green/Pink)
📞 (312) 667-0104 — **WEB:** www.bellemorechicago.com
▪ Closed Saturday - Sunday lunch   **PRICE: $$$**

CABRA 😊

Peruvian • Design

♿ 🚪 🖥 🍹

MAP: E1

Tucked into the 12th floor of the hip Hoxton hotel, this light-soaked and plant-draped stunner overlooks the city's skyline. Its tropical vibe makes the perfect backdrop for Chef Stephanie Izard's wonderfully inventive Peruvian flavors, which she punches up with global touches pulled from her diverse culinary background. Try to grab one of the six seats at the ceviche bar to watch the chefs while they work.

The menu offers ceviches, empanadas, botanas, and anticuchos. The kitchen takes liberties with traditional tastes, producing dishes that celebrate the nation's vibrance and bounty. Don't miss the show-stopping pulpo con olivos—tender octopus paired with avocado, fried capers, and black olive mayo; or smoky goat empanadas coupled with huacatay mayo.

▪ 200 N. Green St. (at Lake St.)
🚇 Morgan
📞 (312) 761-1717 — **WEB:** www.cabrachicago.com
▪ Open lunch & dinner daily   **PRICE: $$**

BLACKBIRD 🏵

Contemporary · Design

In many ways, an acclaimed restaurant that opened in 1997 may seem like old news, but Chef/owner Paul Kahan continues to enliven this Chicago original with fresh talent and new flavor.

The interior is small but packed, right down to the last lunchtime bar stool. Everything feels glossy and white, accented with high-back leather banquettes and orange placemats that pop with color at the bar. Service is sharp, busy and handling it all very well. Begin your unique dining journey here with a warm, poached Maine shrimp salad tossing meaty bacon and pickled walnuts with segments of tangy orange. Then segue into a perfect marriage of salinity and sweetness by way of the ultra-crisp potato-wrapped sturgeon fillet accompanied by tender gnocchi, laid atop a bed of steamed mussels and finished with a luxurious sauce Parisienne. Desserts at Blackbird are equally intricate and inspired, including that divine combination of crunchy apple-cider donuts with creamy cinnamon-laced ricotta, a rich mostarda, as well as a cooling scoop of buckwheat ice cream.

Dinner may be served as a ten-course tasting menu that shows just what this capable kitchen can do. Lunch is an astounding bargain.

🟦 619 W. Randolph St. (bet. Desplaines & Jefferson Sts.)
🚇 Clinton (Green/Pink)
📞 (312) 715-0708 — **WEB:** www.blackbirdrestaurant.com
🟦 Closed Saturday - Sunday lunch   **PRICE: $$$**

CIRA

Mediterranean Cuisine • Design

MAP: E1

This stylish retreat is nestled inside the beautifully designed Hoxton hotel. Its expansive carte roams the cuisines of the countries that flank the Mediterranean sea, including Turkey, North Africa, Spain, and Italy. The result? A veritable feast for the senses. Service is smooth and friendly, making it ideal for both a business lunch and date night.

The menu boasts bright ingredients spun into delicious, shareable dishes, like tomato and cucumber salad mingled with Serrano ham, goat cheese, and hazelnut dukkah. Smoked sablefish with charred asparagus and soft boiled egg is big enough to constitute a full meal, while calamansi posset combining pistachio ice cream, olives, and fresh raspberries is a delightful surprise of flavor and texture.

- 200 N. Green St. (at Lake St.)
- Morgan
- (312) 761-1777 — **WEB:** www.cirachicago.com
- Open lunch & dinner daily

PRICE: $$

EDEN

Contemporary • Chic

MAP: C3

This lovely addition to the West Loop dining scene arrives thanks to husband-and-wife-team, Chef Devon Quinn and Jodi Fyfe. The gorgeous, whitewashed space offers an airy, vibrant ambience even by night, with exposed brick, encaustic tile at the convivial bar, tufted leather banquettes and commissioned artwork throughout.

The inspired cuisine applies flavors of the Mediterranean to seasonal produce, some of it plucked straight from the on-site urban garden. Renowned favorites from the menu may include baked shrimp paccheri; curried lentil brik; or even cumin-grilled lamb with Israeli couscous and merguez. House-made pastas might feature sweet pea pierogi with broccoli purée, trumpet mushrooms, pickled spring onions and crispy potato shards.

- 1748 W. Lake St. (at Wood St.)
- Ashland (Green/Pink)
- (312) 366-2294 — **WEB:** www.edeninchicago.com
- Closed Monday - Tuesday, Wednesday - Saturday lunch, Sunday dinner

PRICE: $$$

157

EL CHE 🍴
Argentinian • *Trendy*

MAP: E2

This love letter to Argentina's cuisine arrives courtesy of Chef John Manion, who spent much of his childhood in Sao Paulo, Brazil and traveling through South America. Look beyond the jade-green tiled exterior to find this cool hot spot. Its slender space is lined with black brick, white mortar and wood slats, and leads to an enormous open-hearth oven in the rear. Tiny votives and potted plants warm the room with an of-the-moment vibe.

Wood-fired grilled dishes figure largely on this menu, where diners may also uncover comfort food favorites like golden-fried empanadas chock-full of spicy beef and sweet golden raisins. Then look forward to morcilla set over a thin purée of white beans and hit with charred shishito peppers for that extra bit of kick.

- 845 W. Washington Blvd. (bet. Green & Peoria Sts.)
- Morgan
- (312) 265-1130 — **WEB:** www.elchechicago.com
- Closed lunch daily

PRICE: $$$

GIBSON'S ITALIA 🍴
Steakhouse • *Elegant*

MAP: F3

There's a reason Gibson's Italia is a see-and-be-seen kind of place. By day, the room is flooded with sunlight and stunning panoramic views of the Chicago River. Come dinnertime, the lights dim and the twinkling cityscape offers romantic magic, while a rooftop bar with fireplace opens up in the summer. And all of that's before you even taste the delicious food.

Much like its sister restaurant in the cheeky «Viagra Triangle, « this Gibson's is an old-school bastion of martinis and red meat. Classics get gussied up with contemporary Italian touches in antipasti plates like the crabmeat and avocado parfait. This menu also features aged Australian grass-fed beef and specialty cuts like the Japanese beef sirloin from the Hyōgo Prefecture, charged by the ounce.

- 233 N. Canal St. (bet. Fulton & Lake Sts.)
- Clinton (Green/Pink)
- (312) 414-1100 — **WEB:** www.gibsonsitalia.com
- Closed Sunday

PRICE: $$$

ELSKE

Contemporary · Design

MAP: C3

A vivid blue neon sign marks the entry to stylish Elske, the hip and sophisticated offering brought to you by husband-and-wife chef duo, David and Anna Posey. He worked at Blackbird; she at The Publican—and what they do together in this restaurant (the name means "love" in Danish) is pure culinary magic.

The spacious setting is equal parts minimal-cool and perfectly cozy, with concrete floors, exposed brick walls, and open ductwork. A lovely outdoor area offers an open-air campfire with two long benches and complimentary lap furs, designed for a pre- or post-dinner cocktail or two. Inside, communal tables abound and counter seats line a gleaming open kitchen, where the cooks serve dishes directly to customers.

The chefs' deeply creative menu offers seasonal, responsibly sourced dishes rendered with impeccable skill—the flavors carefully woven together to produce irresistible profiles. A night in the talented duo's hands might unveil tender duck liver tart in an ethereally light buckwheat crust or subtle-but-noteworthy poached sturgeon and creamed wax beans in a garlic-walnut sauce. Tender venison crowned with plums and sided by ricotta spätzle is spot-on bite after creamy, buttery bite.

🟦 1350 W. Randolph Ave. (at Ada St.)

🚇 Ashland (Green/Pink)

📞 (312) 733-1314 — **WEB:** www.elskerestaurant.com

🟦 Closed Monday - Tuesday, Wednesday - Sunday lunch

PRICE: $$$$

GIRL & THE GOAT
Contemporary • Trendy

MAP: E2

The revolving door never stops turning as Girl & The Goat's party keeps going. Even on a Monday night, guests linger for hours, shouting over the din at this sceney but always friendly stunner. Appropriately rustic wooden pillars and beams connect a warren of seating areas, from elevated platforms to banquettes to dim private corner nooks.

A pick-your-own-protein adventure, the menu is organized by ingredients with a dedicated section for goat. Start with freshly baked ham bread accompanied by smoked Swiss cheese-butter seasoned with coarse mustard and olive tapenade. End with an almost pudding-like "all leches" cake enriched with strawberry-rhubarb sorbet. The kitchen may even send out mini portions of menu items for solo diners—a truly thoughtful touch.

- 809 W. Randolph St. (bet. Green & Halsted Sts.)
- Morgan
- (312) 492-6262 — **WEB:** www.girlandthegoat.com
- Closed lunch daily   **PRICE: $$**

HIGH FIVE RAMEN
Japanese • Rustic

MAP: E2

This repurposed industrial setting is a hipster dining hall serving two hot foodie trends under one roof. The bulk of the sprawling space is devoted to Green Street Smoked Meats, a barbecue joint where crowds of cool kids sit side-by-side downing beers and heaps of pulled pork, brisket and Frito pie.

More worthy of attention, however, is High Five Ramen, a downstairs nook where the queue for one of its 16 seats starts early. Once inside, slurp a bowl of the signature, crazy-spicy broth. Loaded with thin alkaline noodles, a slow-cooked egg, roasted pork belly, locally grown sprouts and black garlic oil, this unique rendition is worth the burn. For sweet, icy relief, sip on a slushy tiki cocktail—then wipe your brow and dig back in.

- 112 N. Green St. (bet. Randolph St. & Washington Blvd.)
- Morgan
- (312) 344-1749 — **WEB:** www.highfiveramen.com
- Closed lunch daily   **PRICE: $**

UNITED

Have a manhattan in Manhattan.

The most flights between Chicago and New York.

fly the friendly skies

KIKKŌ
Asian • Contemporary Décor
🍹

MAP: F1

Kumiko is a luxe cocktail den with an array of seriously crafted bites. However, the stellar attraction is located downstairs, in a secreted away room, featuring deep blue walls as well as a dark stone, ten-seat counter. The team works behind this counter and in front of a backdrop of light wood shelving arranged with pottery, cookbooks, sparkling stemware, and vinyl records.

The beverage program by Julia Momose is serious and highly recommended. Wine and sake are just the beginning, with cocktails raised to a level of artistry here. Several pairings are on offer to accompany the omakase, including a spiritless selection that may lack alcohol but certainly not creativity.

Diners can look forward to a seven-course menu that flirts with Japanese technique, ingredients and flavors, but the unbridled omakase is really designed to enhance the carefully curated drinks list. Get started on sashimi and a few nigiri before moving on to such inventive items as house-made tofu with ramps, pickled green almonds, and an intense dashi. Seared mackerel may be dressed with kombu sabayon, just as A5 Miyazaki Wagyu over nori rice is luxuriously embellished with beef fat hollandaise.

◾ 630 W. Lake St. (at Desplaines St.)

🚇 Clinton

📞 (312) 285-2912 — **WEB:** www.barkumiko.com

◾ Closed Monday - Tuesday, Wednesday - Sunday lunch

PRICE: $$$$

LA JOSIE

Mexican • Contemporary Décor

MAP: E2

You don't want to miss a morsel at this spiffy Mexican charmer. Tucked into a hip space that's both stylish and comfortable, the dining room is flooded with light thanks to floor-to-ceiling windows, and the bar buzzes with energy as bartenders whip up colorful h&rafted cocktails.

La Josie is modern enough where you might expect to find fusion, but this family-run kitchen leans traditional—imagine comforting dishes crafted with pristine ingredients and careful technique. Chef/owner Jose Luis Barajas (AKA Pepe) shows a particularly deft hand in his picture-perfect tacos stuffed with delicious pairings like shredded achiote pork, pickled red onions, and fiery salsa habanero; or tender Amish chicken with crumbled queso fresco and grilled corn kernel salad.

740 W. Randolph St. (at Halstead St.)

Morgan

(312) 929-2900 — **WEB:** www.lajosie.com

Open lunch & dinner daily

PRICE: $$

LA SIRENA CLANDESTINA

Latin American • Rustic

MAP: D1

Chef John Manion may be splitting his time between El Che and his first baby, La Sirena Clandestina, but he hasn't missed a beat. The décor reflects the location's warehouse roots through drafting stools at the bar, well-tread wood plank floors and rugged wood tables edged in steel. Silvery pressed-tin ceilings echo the happy din of conversation below.

Be sure to try the wonderful Brazilian bowl, filled with bomba rice, chimichurri and malagueta chili salsa (good for what ails you with its spicy kick), topped with juicy grilled hangar steak (as well as avocado, grilled chicken, or shrimp). Their empanada is a signature at lunch and dinner; there's even a breakfast version at brunch. Desserts feature a delicious buttermilk tres leches.

954 W. Fulton Market (at Morgan St.)

Morgan

(312) 226-5300 — **WEB:** www.lasirenachicago.com

Closed lunch daily

PRICE: $$

LEÑA BRAVA
Mexican • *Contemporary Décor*

MAP: D2

This prime Randolph Street corner is home to a one-two punch of Rick Bayless-ness—an excellent taqueria and brewery named Cruz Blanza as well as this sophisticated cantina. An open kitchen displaying open-fire cooking is Leña Brava's stimulating focal point, while a buzzing bar pouring an encyclopedic range of agave spirits, brews from next door and rare Mexican wines enhances the bi-level scene.

The kitchen's Northern Mexican-influenced menu combines the bounty of the sea with the primal joy of wood-fired cooking. Be tempted by icy seafood preparations like an aquachile of sashimi-grade diver scallops in spiced cucumber juice. Then consider hearth-roasted black cod al pastor with sweet and sour pineapple, coupled with heirloom corn tortillas.

- 900 W. Randolph St. (at Peoria St.)
- Morgan
- (312) 733-1975 — **WEB:** www.rickbayless.com
- Closed Monday, Tuesday - Sunday lunch　　**PRICE: $$$**

LOU MITCHELL'S
American • *Historic*

MAP: F5

Strategically set near Union Station, this American institution is beloved by all and sundry. Not only has it stood the test of time—since 1923 to be exact—but thanks to its first-rate comfort food and inviting vibe, it is routinely packed with diners jonesing for classics and signatures.

The menu has something for everyone, including soups, chowders, and even a Dutch oven-pot roast or sloppy Joes with coleslaw. Of course, when it comes to grilling, this kitchen is king. Case in point: La Conga Delight, which reveals just the right dot of decadence via slices of buttery brioche stuffed with bacon, tomato, and cheese. Pies and cakes are crafted daily and worth the splurge, especially that dense and creamy chocolate layer cake with frosting to boot.

- 565 W. Jackson Blvd. (bet. Clinton & Jefferson Sts.)
- Clinton (Blue)
- (312) 939-3111 — **WEB:** www.loumitchellsrestaurant.com
- Closed dinner daily　　**PRICE: $**

MAKO ✿

Japanese · Elegant

After making a name for his tasting menus at Lincoln Park's Juno, veteran sushi chef B. K. Park has spun out this inspiring shrine to omakase. With nothing but a single plaque marking its entrance, this Japanese gem can be tough to spot. But once inside its tranquil dining room, the surrounding din of roaring traffic fades into the background and you'll be entirely transfixed by the chef's dedication to the sushi craft.

Mako is a hot ticket, with just 22 seats in which to savor the smartly considered omakase, featuring black sea bream wrapped around ankimo; pickled chayote crowned with a micro fava leaf; Osetra caviar; as well as king crab with uni miso, A5 Wagyu butter, and a potato chip. Equally enticing are its seasonal sushi and cooked dishes, like poached abalone braised with soy sauce and finished with just the right brush of XO sauce; as well as sea bass with charred frisée and seaweed. Not to be outdone, artistically presented chutoro and smoked salmon sashimi flaunt ace flavor and flawless texture. Chawanmushi stocked with mushroom and crab is the very essence of classic refinement.

Dessert is not an afterthought, as seen in sweet potato with whiskey caramel and crème Diplomat.

■ 731 W. Lake St. (bet. Halsted St. & Union Ave.)

🚇 Morgan

✆ (312) 988-0687 — **WEB:** www.makochicago.com

■ Closed Monday, Tuesday -Sunday lunch   **PRICE: $$$$**

MAUDE'S LIQUOR BAR 🍴

French • Cozy

🍹 ♿ 🏠 🛋 🍸

It's impossible not to love this place. The overstuffed curio cabinet and blue French metal chairs aren't true antiques, for this gorgeously disheveled and rather classy brasserie isn't as old as the mirror's arful patina would have you believe. A handsome bar mixing contemporary and classic cocktails adds to the vintage atmosphere.

Fill up on French comfort food under the glow of mismatched crystal chandeliers, or head to the second-floor bar to snack on oysters and frites. The Lyonnaise salad is downright beautiful, tossing escarole, frisée and baby romaine in chive vinaigrette beneath a soft boiled egg and chunks of grilled pork belly. Steak tartare satisfies from beginning to end, and the crème brûlée makes for a deliciously textbook finish.

◾ 840 W. Randolph St. (bet. Green & Peoria Sts.)
🚇 Morgan
📞 (312) 243-9712 — **WEB:** www.maudesliquorbar.com
◾ Closed Sunday - Monday, Tuesday - Saturday lunch **PRICE: $$**

MOMOTARO 🍴

Japanese • Design

🍹 🍶 🛋 🍸

Boka Restaurant Group's stunning West Loop canteen embraces a fantastical view of Japanese dining. An impressive selection of imported whiskies is listed on a retro-style departure board; a private dining room upstairs is styled to resemble a mid-century corporate boardroom; and a traditional izakaya beckons diners downstairs. Consistently packed, this impeccably designed space boasts numerous kitchens churning out a range of dishes.

Jidori kimo, those prized chicken oysters—here grilled to perfection—has long been a signature, while the beef tsukune sliders in a bao from the robata-yaki are equally impressive. Don't miss the delicious nigiri or maki, including una-kyu or the ebi uni maguro, of which there are only ten per evening, so plan ahead.

◾ 820 W. Lake St. (at Green St.)
🚇 Morgan
📞 (312) 733-4818 — **WEB:** www.momotarochicago.com
◾ Closed lunch daily
PRICE: $$$

MONTEVERDE

Italian · *Trendy*

MAP: E4

Chef Sarah Grueneberg is a local celebrity, so expect her offspring to be packed to the last dining counter stool by 5:30 P. M. Then again this is prime seating, because behind that wood-grain bar lies the pasta station where sheets are rolled, cut, and hung to dry. Her signature Italian cooking—or cucina tipica as the menu lists it—is what draws crowds.

That said, this menu is about more than just pasta, beginning with an extraordinary yet humble vessel displaying bundles of cabbage leaves stuffed with herbed breadcrumbs, mushrooms, and porcini Bolognese. Subbing whey for water in the cacio whey pepe delivers a slight tang and added creaminess, and the al dente pasta, tossed in Pecorino Romano and finished with a four peppercorn blend, is spot on.

- 1020 W. Madison St. (at Carpenter St.)
- Morgan
- (312) 888-3041 — **WEB:** www.monteverdechicago.com
- Closed Monday, Tuesday - Sunday lunch   **PRICE: $$**

PROXI ☺

International · *Contemporary Décor*

MAP: F2

Here at Proxi, Chef Andrew Zimmerman seems intent on presenting his diners with a culinary whirlwind that blows from Thai beef salad to coal-roasted oysters with ssamjang butter and beyond. Otherworldly highlights reveal delicate duck dumplings floating in a pho broth with fried shallots and aromatic herbs. Regardless of the dish's inspiration, it's sure to be delicious in this kitchen's capable hands. Desserts, like avocado mousse, are made with formidable talent.

The massive room is effortlessly cool and sleek, with blue-tiled columns set beneath the white-vaulted ceiling. It also features an open kitchen and myriad seating options for everyone—from solo diners to large groups. A front lounge is ideal for lingering and waiting for your party to arrive.

- 565 W. Randolph St. (at Jefferson St.)
- Clinton (Green/Pink)
- (312) 466-1950 — **WEB:** www.proxichicago.com
- Closed Sunday, Monday - Saturday lunch   **PRICE: $$**

NEXT

Contemporary • Trendy

MAP: D1

Whether you come to experience the cuisine of ancient Rome, Hollywood, or even The World's 50 Best (whereby Next serves as a cover band by replicating the greatest hits from restaurants that put chefs on the global map), the experience here is pure dinner theater. These culinary themes are not just unique, but also very thoughtful, having the full house of happy crowds waiting with bated breath to see what's "next."

This year began with Silk & Spice, through which diners were taken on a sensory joyride, starting with "mole and rain" combining a cube of rosy pork belly with red mole sauce, followed by the playful "glass canvas" starring strategically set bowls of spices and grains meant to be mixed and matched with accompaniments like beef, parsnip, and shallot confit. The Italia menu came later, during which complex ingredients, flawless flavors, and extraordinary textures were united in classics like cacio e pepe, guanciale-wrapped branzino with a vibrant quartet of condiments, as well as veal cheek agrodolce served atop a savory bread pudding.

Fully vested servers display an encyclopedic knowledge of each prevailing topic as well as the reason for their coming into being.

---

953 W. Fulton Market (at Morgan St.)

Morgan

N/A — **WEB:** www.nextrestaurant.com

Closed Monday - Tuesday, Wednesday - Sunday lunch

PRICE: $$$$

OMAKASE YUME ✿

Japanese • Intimate

The subtleties behind Yume's entrance—marked by a basic black awning—along with its particularly skillful preparations allow it to stand tall and loom large over its more extravagant competitors.

Equally spartan in décor, this small and clean dining enclave (brought to you by Chef/owner Sangtae Park) is lined with planks of pale blonde wood and offers two nightly seatings at its pristine eight-seat bar, attended to by a few graceful servers. Light beats in the background keep the mood from being too sterile.

Dishes tend to headline top ingredients that are both smartly paired and well executed. Savor the chef's unfaltering focus on Japanese cuisine by way of deep-fried nasu hirame; Edo-style sushi featuring madai, akami, and chutoro; as well as slices of Wagyu beef, brushed with soy, and finished with grated wasabi. Other delicacies like torigai (heart clam), ultra-seasonal and correctly aged sayori, or even grilled misoyaki over rice flaunt a thorough study in product sourcing, fresh flavors, and delectable textures. Sweet and custardy tamago, followed by matcha panna cotta—deeply colorful, full-bodied and tart with creamy buttermilk—bring the meal to a close.

■ 651 W. Washington Blvd. (bet. Desplaines St. & Warren Ave.)

🚇 Clinton St

✆ (312) 265-1610 — **WEB:** www.omakaseyume.com

■ Closed Sunday, Monday - Saturday lunch   **PRICE: $$$$**

ORIOLE ✿ ✿
Contemporary · Elegant

⌘ ♿

Welcome to one of Chicago's greatest restaurants. The interior is mod yet industrial, with an open kitchen—filled with jovial professionals who look like they're cooking for a dinner party—that takes up a good deal of the space. The fact that nothing feels stuffy should not surprise since Oriole is something of a family business. Crisp attention to detail is clear from every member of this team, who are all thoroughly versed in the intricacies of the rather complex menu.

Oriole's tasting menu is stimulating and utterly contemporary; borderless with its interweaving of global flavors. It all begins with a cavalcade of delicate small bites: Aged hamachi with fresh wasabi and truffle honey shows a fascinating sweetness. Maine uni with yuzu kosho and puffed rice has fantastic crunch. A single crab shumai bobs in a soothing kabocha and ginger broth. Caraway cappellini is paired with a rich yeast butter, puffed wheat, and shaved black truffle for a heady dish. Desserts offer a tempting array from a celery-pistachio financier and guava Danish to sweet potato cheesecake and peppermint-dark chocolate bon bon.

Oriole thinks of everything; there is even a non-alcoholic beverage pairing on offer.

■ 661 W. Walnut St. (at Union Ave.)

🚇 Clinton (Green/Pink)

✆ (312) 877-5339 — WEB: www.oriolechicago.com

■ Closed Sunday - Monday, Tuesday - Saturday lunch

PRICE: $$$$

THE PUBLICAN ∦○
Gastropub • *Tavern*

MAP: E1

Everything about this local gem screams happy place—and scream you might have to, but the noisy din is all part of the fun. Inside, find a dining concept based on century-old public houses marked by equal parts lively conversations and pours of beer. Each item on the menu lists its place of origin next to it: cobia caught in Destin, FL; or lettuce grown in Buckley, MI. Global flavors make a guest appearance too, like jamón Serrano from Salamanca, Spain. Portraits of pigs hang in the room, and sure enough, braised pork belly flash-fried and laid over a sunchoke purée with blanched fava beans makes for a spectacular finish.

Bargain hunters should come at lunch for the Pub-fixe or specialty lunch board with charcuterie, bread, and cheese.

- 837 W. Fulton Market (at Green St.)
- Morgan
- (312) 733-9555 — **WEB:** www.thepublicanrestaurant.com
- Open lunch & dinner daily   **PRICE: $$$**

ROISTER ∦○
Contemporary • *Rustic*

MAP: D1

Unapologetically loud and laid-back, Roister is part of Chef Grant Achatz's culinary campus, though the cooking here is far more rustic. Boldly incorporated into the dining room, the kitchen serves as the focal point—with the best seats at the counter, facing the blazing hearth. As expected, the food is creative and modern, but also soulful in incorporating the wood fire. Start with the likes of hearth-roasted rainbow carrots served with smoked labneh and pistachio croutons, before lingering over deliciously crusted salmon. In lieu of dessert, go for the baked Swiss cheese puff topped with sweet pear and peppery watercress.

Brunch is hard to pass up, with crispy chicken and waffles slathered in honey butter and drizzled with whiskey syrup.

- 951 W. Fulton Market (bet. Morgan & Sangamon Sts.)
- Morgan
- (312) 789-4896 — **WEB:** www.roisterrestaurant.com
- Closed Monday - Thursday lunch   **PRICE: $$$**

ROOH

Indian • Design

MAP: E2

This bright and beautiful setting, located at the edge of the crowded dining strip of West Randolph, is spread over two floors and outfitted with deep blue velvet seats. Libations poured here have their own flavor matrix—study them if you must but rest assured that all are great.

Similarly, the menu is dotted with Indian classics enhanced by such cutting-edge flavors as seen in the deep-fried cauliflower koliwada, accompanied by tempered yogurt and a rice mousse with peanut thecha. Follow this up with hearty beef short rib curry stocked with carrots and marrow kofta. Classic palates will relish the wonderfully creamy dal coupled with a plain naan for scooping, while a baked semolina cake with milk ice cream and pistachios will have sweet teeth swooning.

- 736 W. Randolph St. (near Halsted St.)
- Morgan
- (312) 267-2323 — **WEB:** www.roohchicago.com
- Closed Monday, Tuesday - Sunday lunch

PRICE: $$$

SUSHI DOKKU

Japanese • Neighborhood

MAP: E2

Creatively adorned, Americanized nigiri is the featured attraction at this hip sushi-ya that's all wood planks, stainless steel, chunky tables, and hefty benches.

Why just have one piece when you can have two? Here, each order is served in pairs. Among the selection, enjoy the likes of hamachi sporting a spicy mix of shredded Napa cabbage, daikon, and red chili; or salmon dressed with a sweet ginger-soy sauce and fried ginger chips. South Pacific sea bream is deliciously embellished with a drizzle of smoky tomato and black sea salt. Those who wish to branch out opt for takoyaki (crispy fried octopus croquettes) or grilled hamachi collar. To finish, try the brownie-crusted green tea-cheesecake or Fuji Fu apple cake with peanuts and caramel sauce.

- 823 W. Randolph St. (at Green St.)
- Morgan
- (312) 455-8238 — **WEB:** www.sushidokku.com
- Closed Sunday - Monday, Saturday lunch

PRICE: $$

SEPIA

American • Vintage

Housed within a historical 19th-century print shop, this urbane, stylish but unfussy dining room does a fine job mixing original details with modern touches. Muted tones in the exposed brick walls and custom tile floors complement newer elements like floor-to-ceiling wine storage and dramatic smoke-shaded chandeliers that drip with crystals.

Though the décor may tip its hat to yesteryear, the ambience is decidedly inviting and Chef Andrew Zimmerman's cuisine is firmly grounded in the present.

Settle into one of their spacious tables and look forward to a meal that reflects the delicious amalgam of American cuisine, with hints of Southeast Asian, Korean and Mediterranean tastes. But, it is at dinner when this kitchen truly shines. Gnocchi for instance may seem commonplace, but this version is memorable thanks to the flawless components and rich flavors of lamb sugo and ciabatta breadcrumbs. Chicken is downright exciting, served crisp-skinned with a buttery Albufera sauce, crumbly chestnuts, caramelized fennel and sausage. Simple-sounding desserts keep the bar high until the very end of the feast, and may include a toffee-coconut cake with chocolate ganache and burnt caramel.

- 123 N. Jefferson St. (bet. Randolph St. & Washington Blvd.)
- Clinton (Green/Pink)
- (312) 441-1920 — **WEB:** www.sepiachicago.com
- Closed Saturday - Sunday lunch   **PRICE:** $$$

SMYTH ✿✿

Contemporary • Elegant

MAP: D4

Housed in what looks like an unremarkable industrial building, find a setting worthy of interior design magazine covers. Once inside, head up the few stairs to arrive at Smyth; then proceed into a space, which feels so comfortable that it's easy to forget you're in a restaurant. The service staff is hospitable, down to earth and manages to keep the ambience relaxed despite Chefs John Shields and Karen Urie Shields' intense craftsmanship. Beyond, the open kitchen mixes white tiles and cutting-edge equipment with a roaring hearth fire. There is a "come as you are" feeling among the crowd here, but everyone has dressed up a bit, as if in deference to the superb meal that awaits them. Original, and at times even pleasantly experimental, this kitchen's cooking has a clear vision that is sure to meet every expectation of its versatile diners. Some dishes deliver surprises through strong and gutsy flavor combinations, like a well-aged ribeye rubbed with yeasty Marmite. Other menu items strive for subtlety, such as the dried pear "jerky."

Creativity reaches its height in the "milk chocolate" dessert, which is more of a brilliant umami-bomb than confection, served with huckleberries and shiitakes.

■ 177 N. Ada St. (bet. Lake & Randolph Sts.)
🚇 Ashland (Green/Pink)
✆ (773) 913-3773 — **WEB:** www.smythandtheloyalist.com
■ Closed Sunday - Monday, Tuesday - Saturday lunch

PRICE: $$$$

SWIFT & SONS 🍴

Steakhouse • Elegant

With the inception of this large steakhouse at 1K Fulton, New York City-based design firm AvroKO adds to their local portfolio in collaboration with the Boka Restaurant Group. A renovated meat and produce warehouse built in the 1920s, this space unwinds from a raw bar aptly named Cold Storage into a plush hangout. Here, striking wood-trimmed arches and concrete columns modulate the scale of the rooms.

The kitchen's contemporary take on steak serves up USDA Prime beef seared at high heat and presented with a trio of sauces. It's the kind of place where gluttony is rewarded—even the wine list features Coravin selections in three- or six-ounce pours. Extras (like king crab Oscar) or desserts (like Boston cream pie) are worth the calories.

■ 1000 W. Fulton Market (at Morgan St.)
🚇 Morgan
✆ (312) 733-9420 — **WEB:** www.swiftandsonschicago.com
■ Closed lunch daily   **PRICE: $$$$**

Remember, stars ✿
are awarded for cuisine only! Elements
such as service and décor are not a factor.

YŪGEN ✿

Contemporary · Elegant

& ♿

MAP: F2

Its entrance is unassuming, but one step inside this vast arena— punctuated by natural hues, abstract art, and luxuriously spaced tables—and you'll find yourself enveloped in elegance. The best seats in the house are those with views of the open kitchen, where Chef Mari Katsumura and her team can be seen preparing and delivering thoughtfully composed meals.

Begin with such crowning canapes as king crab with hollandaise or a texturally exquisite duo of both raw and fried seaweed coupled with creamed celery root. This may be tailed by luscious yellowtail sashimi; still warm Norwegian fjord trout; fluffly crab rice studded with confit egg yolk; or even okara agnolotti with wild huckleberries. Seal the regal meal with a plate of "Milk & Cookies" unveiling hōjicha ice cream that's covered in buttermilk foam and then topped with thin shards of crisp meringue as well as a thick swipe of caramelized milk.

But wait, there's more. The wine list offers sake by the glass, including a trio of namazake (unpasteurized selections) to celebrate the arrival of spring. And speaking of inventive sips, cocktail fans should stop by Kaisho—the chic front bar room serving seasonal concoctions and light bites.

■ 652 W. Randolph St. (bet. Desplaines & Halstead Sts.)
℘ (312) 265-1008 — **WEB:** www.yugenchicago.com
■ Closed Sunday - Monday, Tuesday - Saturday lunch

INDEXES

ALPHABETICAL LIST OF RESTAURANTS

RESTAURANTS BY CUISINE

RESTAURANTS BY NEIGHBORHOOD

CHINATOWN & SOUTH _____

GOLD COAST _____

RIVER NORTH

WEST LOOP

RESTAURANTS BY NEIGHBORHOOD

STARRED RESTAURANTS

✿ ✿ ✿ _____

BIB GOURMAND